P9-CQI-784

Civil War
Battles and Leaders

Civil War

Battles and Leaders

AARON R. MURRAY, EDITOR

DK Publishing, Inc.

LONDON, NEW YORK, MUNICH,
MELBOURNE, AND DELHI

DK PUBLISHING, INC.
Senior Editor Beth Sutinis
Assistant Managing Art Editor Michelle Baxter
Associate Editor Elizabeth Hester
Creative Director Tina Vaughan
Jacket Art Director Dirk Kaufman
Publisher Chuck Lang
Production Manager Chris Avgherinos

MEDIA PROJECTS INC.
Executive Editor Carter Smith
Editor Aaron R. Murray
Contributing Writer Stuart Murray
Consultants Brian Pohanka, Don Troiani
Designer Laura Smyth, Smythtype
Production Editor James Burmester
Copy Editor Kristen Behrens

First American Edition, 2004
05 06 10 9 8 7 6 5 4 3 2

Published in the United States
by DK Publishing, Inc.
375 Hudson Street
New York, New York 10014

Copyright © 2004 DK Publishing, Inc.
All rights reserved under International and Pan-
American Copyright Conventions. No part of
this publication may be reproduced, stored in a
retrieval system, or transmitted in any form or
by any means, electronic, mechanical,
photocopying, recording, or otherwise, without
the prior written permission of the
copyright owner.

A catalog record for this book is available
from the Library of Congress.

ISBN 0-7894-9891-X (PB)
ISBN 0-7894-9890-1 (HC)

Reproduced by Colourscan, Singapore
Printed and bound in China by
South China Printing Co., Ltd.

Discover more at

www.dk.com

*Halftitle: Robert E. Lee mounted on his horse
Traveller. Title page: Charge of Union troops at
The Battle of Cold Harbor in Virginia.*

CONTENTS

GENERAL P.G.T. BEAUREGARD'S EPAULETS

**21ST ILLINOIS
REGIMENTAL BUGLE**

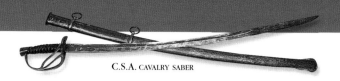

C.S.A. CAVALRY SABER

CONFEDERATE BATTLE FLAG,
ALABAMA REGIMENT

1863: HIGH TIDE FOR THE CONFEDERACY *44*

20TH MAINE BATTLEFIELD PAROLE

1864: TOTAL WAR IN THE CONFEDERACY *64*

SHRAPNEL-DENTED UNION DRINKING CUP

1865: GRANT TRAPS LEE, PURSUIT TO APPOMATTOX *86*

WAR BETWEEN THE STATES

To Northerners it was the Civil War or the War of the Rebellion. Southerners called it the War of Southern Independence. The North fought to save the Union, the South to create a new nation.

In 1861, most Americans did not know what war was. They had lived in peace so long that the wars and battles they heard about seemed like adventure stories. That changed after Confederates in South Carolina fired at Fort Sumter on April 12.

For years there had been conflict in the land. Northern states were growing in industry and population, gaining power in Congress. The rural South depended on African-American slavery, which many Northerners despised and wanted to abolish. Southerners demanded more power for the individual states and called for the expansion of slavery into new territories.

Newly elected President Abraham Lincoln was a Northerner. Southern firebrands believed he was an enemy. Their states seceded from the Union to create an independent nation: the Confederate States of America (C.S.A.). The North and Lincoln swore to

REINFORCING THE LINE
Federal troops and horse artillery rush forward to prevent a C.S.A. breakthrough at Gettysburg in July 1863. General Winfield S. Hancock (center) orders his men forward in the battle that swept back the "high tide" of the Confederacy's invasion of the North.

preserve the Union, and the stage was set for civil war. Neither side imagined the other would fight so relentlessly. Neither guessed the immense price in human life. In four years of conflict, more than 622,000 Americans died in this "War Between the States," as it was also called.

Just three counties in northern Virginia were fought over by half a million men during the war. Among those who died in that small space were 19 generals—10 Union and nine Confederate. The Civil War's leaders were sure to be in the place of greatest danger. Generals directed attacks as

enemy bullets whizzed around them. Colonels drew swords and led charges. Many brave commanders were killed or wounded. After the war, they were long remembered by the men they led into battle.

STUDYING MAPS, MAKING PLANS
Union General-in-Chief Ulysses S. Grant leans over a bench during a council of war with his staff and commanding generals.

AMERICANS CHOOSE SIDES

THE COMMANDER-IN-CHIEF
Lincoln confers with McClellan after the Battle of Antietam in September 1862. Lincoln urged McClellan to pursue the withdrawing Confederates. When McClellan moved too slowly, Lincoln relieved him.

FLAG OF THE 54TH
The 54th Massachusetts was one of the first all-black regiments raised by the Union. More than 300,000 African-Americans served in the Union army and navy during the war.

In early 1861, the U.S. Army had only 16,300 officers and men, most serving on the western frontier. Others were in lonely outposts on the Canadian border or in coastal forts. The U.S. Navy was just strong enough to defend the coasts. There was no need for anything more.

The victory over Mexico in 1846–1847 had given America a new set of heroes, though most had left the military by 1861. Some, like Robert E. Lee and James Longstreet, remained in the service as career officers. Others, such as Ulysses S. Grant and George B. McClellan, went into private business. The general-in-chief of the army was the elderly Winfield Scott, a hero of both the War of 1812 and the Mexican War.

Scott's officer corps numbered 1,080 as civil war approached, but 286 resigned and entered the Confederate service. Active officers who were graduates of the U.S. Military Academy at West Point numbered 824. Of these, 184 went to the South. Of the 900 West Point graduates in civilian life, 114 returned to fight for the Union, while 99 joined the Confederate army. The navy had 1,300 officers, and 322 resigned to join the Confederacy. Of the 287 U.S. Naval Academy graduates in the service, 60 joined the South.

West Pointers dominated the lists of generals on both sides: 194 Confederate, 294 Federal. Yet, at the start, none had ever led an army in battle. Graduates of the military academy would command both sides in 55 of the war's 60 major engagements, and one side in the remaining five engagements.

In that momentous spring of 1861, the officers shook hands with one another and said good-bye. They knew their next meeting might be across a battlefield. The loyalty of these leaders to their home states reflects how people felt all across the nation. As war clouds gathered, many left their adopted states—North and South—and went home to defend the state of their birth.

The population of the 33 states and territories of the United States was 31.4 million in 1861. Approximately 23 million lived in the 22 Northern states. The 9 million people in the Southern states included 3.5 million African-American slaves.

In the course of the war, the Union put 2.1 million men into uniform. Of

BATTALION FLAG
This C.S.A silk flank marker flag helped show officers where their troops were positioned.

these, 500,000 were foreign-born, with the largest groups being 175,000 from Germany and 150,000 from Ireland. Figures for the total Confederate forces or their makeup are not known.

Whether a soldier in the Civil War was native-born or an immigrant, African-American or American Indian, he was known to his opponents as "Billy Yank" or "Johnny Reb." The Yankees and Rebels of 1861–1865 faithfully supported the causes they believed in. They fought and died, won and lost, and changed America and Americans forever.

OBSERVING THE BATTLE
General Robert E. Lee, field glasses in hand, watches from a hilltop as his victory unfolds at Fredericksburg in December 1862.

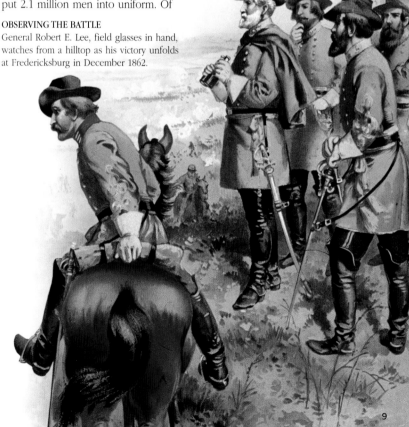

A TIME OF WAR

1861

JANUARY South Carolina, Mississippi, Florida, Alabama, Georgia, Louisiana, and Texas secede from the Union

FEBRUARY Jefferson Davis elected president of the Confederacy • Confederates seize Federal forts

MARCH Abraham Lincoln is inaugurated president of the United States

APRIL Confederates fire on Fort Sumter, South Carolina • Virginia secedes • Massachusetts Regiment is attacked by Baltimore mob • Lincoln declares naval blockade of southern ports

MAY North Carolina and Arkansas secede

JUNE Tennessee secedes • West Virginia breaks off from Virginia • Slave states Delaware, Kentucky, Maryland, and Missouri stay in Union

JULY First Battle of Bull Run, Virginia • Union commander General Irvin McDowell is replaced by General George McClellan

AUGUST Battle of Wilson's Creek, Missouri

NOVEMBER Lincoln appoints McClellan general-in-chief • Union Navy captures Port Royal, South Carolina

1862

FEBRUARY General Ulysses S. Grant captures Fort Henry and Fort Donelson in Tennessee

MARCH Battle of Pea Ridge, Arkansas • Union ironclad warship USS *Monitor* battles Confederate ironclad CSS *Virginia* to a draw • McClellan begins advance against Richmond

APRIL Siege of Yorktown, Virginia • Battle of Shiloh, Tennessee • Union Navy captures New Orleans, Louisiana

BATTLE OF SHILOH

MAY Jackson's Valley Campaign begins • Corinth, Mississippi captured by the Union • Battle of Fair Oaks, Virginia

JUNE Robert E. Lee takes command of the Confederate Army of Northern Virginia • Seven Days' Battles, Virginia

JULY Lincoln appoints General Henry Halleck general-in-chief of Union armies

AUGUST Second Battle of Bull Run, Virginia

SEPTEMBER Battle of Chantilly, Virginia • Lee invades Maryland • Battles of South Mountain, Maryland and Crampton's Gap, Maryland • Jackson captures Harpers Ferry, West Virginia • Battle of Antietam, Maryland • Lincoln issues the Emancipation Proclamation

OCTOBER C.S.A. forces invade Kentucky • Battle of Perryville, Kentucky • General Don Carlos Buell replaced by General William Rosecrans in Kentucky

NOVEMBER Lincoln replaces McClellan with General Ambrose Burnside

DECEMBER Battle of Fredericksburg, Virginia • Battle of Stones River, Tennessee begins

USS *MONITOR* FIGHTS CSS *VIRGINIA*

1863

JANUARY Battle of Stones River continues • Lincoln replaces Burnside with General Joseph Hooker • Grant takes command of the Army of the West

MAY Battle of Chancellorsville, Virginia • Stonewall Jackson killed • Siege of Vicksburg, Mississippi begins

JUNE Cavalry battle at Brandy Station, Virginia • Lee invades the North • Lincoln replaces Hooker with General George Meade

JULY Battle of Gettysburg, Pennsylvania • Vicksburg surrenders • Port Hudson, Louisiana surrenders • Union attack on Fort Wagner, South Carolina fails • Draft riots in Northern cities

SEPTEMBER Battle of Chickamauga, Georgia • Union army trapped at Chattanooga, Tennessee

NOVEMBER Lincoln delivers the Gettysburg Address • Grant breaks siege of Chattanooga • Siege of Knoxville, Tennessee begins

1864

USS KEARSARGE FIGHTS CSS ALABAMA

FEBRUARY Sherman begins campaign against Meridian, Mississippi

MARCH Red River Campaign begins in Louisiana • Lincoln appoints Grant commander of all Union armies • Sherman succeeds Grant as commander of the Army of the West

APRIL Battle of Sabine Cross Roads, Louisiana • Battle of Pleasant Hill, Louisiana • Fort Pillow, Tennessee falls

MAY With Battle of the Wilderness, Virginia, Grant opens a war of attrition, wearing down C.S.A. forces • Sherman's Atlanta campaign begins from Chattanooga, Tennessee • Battle of Spotsylvania Court House, Virginia • Union general John Sedgwick is killed • Sheridan leads a raid on Richmond • Battle of Yellow Tavern, Virginia • C.S.A. cavalry commander Jeb Stuart is killed • Colonel Joseph Bailey dams the Red River and saves Union gunboat fleet • Battle of Resaca, Georgia • Battle of New Market, Virginia • Battle of North Anna, Virginia

PORT HUDSON ON THE MISSISSIPPI

JUNE Battle of Cold Harbor, Virginia • Battle of Brice's Crossroads, Mississippi • Siege of Petersburg, Virginia begins • USS *Kearsarge* sinks CSS *Alabama,* off the coast of Cherbourg, France • Battle of Kennesaw Mountain, Georgia

JULY C.S.A. general Jubal Early raids into Maryland, threatening Washington, D.C. • C.S.A. commander General John B. Hood replaces General Joseph E. Johnston defending Atlanta against Sherman • Battle of Peach Tree Creek, Georgia • Battle of Atlanta, Georgia • Battle of the Crater, Virginia

AUGUST Battle of Mobile Bay, Alabama

SEPTEMBER Fall of Atlanta to Union troops • Sheridan's Shenandoah Valley Campaign begins

OCTOBER Battle of Allatoona, Georgia • Battle of Cedar Creek, Virginia

NOVEMBER Hood's Franklin-Nashville Campaign begins • Lincoln is reelected • Sherman begins March to the Sea • Battle of Franklin, Tennessee

DECEMBER Battle of Nashville, Tennessee • Fall of Savannah, Georgia

1865

LEE SURRENDERS AT APPOMATTOX COURT HOUSE

JANUARY Congress approves 13th Amendment to the Constitution, abolishing slavery • Sherman's Carolina campaign begins

MARCH Lincoln's second inauguration

APRIL Grant breaks through Lee's lines at Petersburg • C.S.A. general A.P. Hill is killed in defense of Petersburg • Battle of Five Forks, Virginia • Richmond is occupied by Union troops • Sheridan cuts off Lee's army at Appomattox Court House, Virginia • Lee surrenders to Grant at Appomattox Court House • John Wilkes Booth assassinates Lincoln at Ford Theater in Washington • Johnston surrenders to Sherman in North Carolina

MAY C.S.A. general Richard Taylor surrenders to Union general Edward Canby in Alabama • General Edmund Kirby Smith surrenders all C.S.A. forces west of the Mississippi to Canby

THE PATHS OF WAR

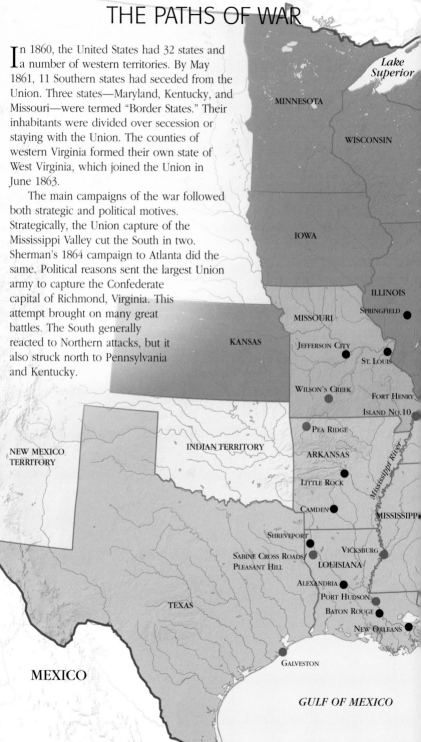

In 1860, the United States had 32 states and a number of western territories. By May 1861, 11 Southern states had seceded from the Union. Three states—Maryland, Kentucky, and Missouri—were termed "Border States." Their inhabitants were divided over secession or staying with the Union. The counties of western Virginia formed their own state of West Virginia, which joined the Union in June 1863.

The main campaigns of the war followed both strategic and political motives. Strategically, the Union capture of the Mississippi Valley cut the South in two. Sherman's 1864 campaign to Atlanta did the same. Political reasons sent the largest Union army to capture the Confederate capital of Richmond, Virginia. This attempt brought on many great battles. The South generally reacted to Northern attacks, but it also struck north to Pennsylvania and Kentucky.

Lake Superior

MINNESOTA

WISCONSIN

IOWA

ILLINOIS

SPRINGFIELD

MISSOURI

KANSAS

JEFFERSON CITY

ST. LOUIS

WILSON'S CREEK

FORT HENRY

ISLAND NO. 10

PEA RIDGE

NEW MEXICO TERRITORY

INDIAN TERRITORY

ARKANSAS

Mississippi River

LITTLE ROCK

CAMDEN

MISSISSIPPI

SHREVEPORT

VICKSBURG

SABINE CROSS ROADS

PLEASANT HILL

LOUISIANA

ALEXANDRIA

PORT HUDSON

TEXAS

BATON ROUGE

NEW ORLEANS

MEXICO

GALVESTON

GULF OF MEXICO

UNITED STATES
CONFEDERATE STATES
BORDER STATES
TERRITORIES
● BATTLE SITE
● TOWN OR FORT

MAINE

CANADA

Lake Huron

Lake Ontario

VERMONT

NEW HAMPSHIRE

NEW YORK

MASSACHUSETTS

● BOSTON

MICHIGAN

Lake Michigan

Lake Erie

CONN.   R.I.

NEW YORK

PENNSYLVANIA

NEW JERSEY

OHIO

Harrisburg

Gettysburg

● PHILADELPHIA

INDIANA

COLUMBUS

HARPERS FERRY

Antietam

DELAWARE

BULL RUN (1ST, 2ND)

Washington, D.C.

MARYLAND

BRANDY STATION

CHANCELLORSVILLE, THE WILDERNESS

FREDERICKSBURG

SPOTSYLVANIA COURT HOUSE

COLD HARBOR, SEVEN DAYS' BATTLES

LOUISVILLE   FRANKFURT

WEST VIRGINIA

LEXINGTON

Richmond

HAMPTON ROADS

PERRYVILLE

APPOMATTOX

PETERSBURG, FIVE FORKS

KENTUCKY

VIRGINIA

FORT DONELSON   KNOXVILLE

NORTH CAROLINA

ATLANTIC OCEAN

TENNESSEE

NASHVILLE

STONES RIVER

● CHARLOTTE

FRANKLIN   CHATTANOOGA

SHILOH   CHICKAMAUGA

SOUTH CAROLINA

WILMINGTON

FORT FISHER

KENNESAW MOUNTAIN

Columbia

ATLANTA

CHARLESTON/ FORT SUMTER

ALABAMA

GEORGIA

Port Royal

SAVANNAH

MONTGOMERY

MOBILE   TALLAHASSEE

FLORIDA

CONFEDERATE CANNONEER

13

First Clashes on the Road to War

The United States was falling apart in January 1861, as the Southern states seceded from the Union. Newly elected President Abraham Lincoln pleaded for national unity.

"A house divided against itself cannot stand," Lincoln said, but secession continued.

Southerners founded the Confederate States of America (C.S.A), established on their own principles and institutions. One principle was the right of states to be free of federal interference. One important institution was enslavement of African-Americans.

Most Northerners believed the Union must be held together at all costs. Many also opposed slavery. Americans on both sides were prepared to fight for their causes.

C.S.A. president Jefferson Davis demanded that U.S. troops evacuate

SUMTER UNDER FIRE Confederate artillery pounds Fort Sumter into a smoking rubble on April 12, 1861, starting the Civil War. North and South mobilized for what most Americans expected would be a short war.

November	March	April	July
Confederate States of America formed with Jefferson Davis as president	Abraham Lincoln sworn in as president of the United States of America	Confederates open fire on Fort Sumter, South Carolina Lincoln calls for 75,000 volunteer soldiers to put down the rebellion	First Bull Run (First Manassas) George B. McClellan takes command of the Army of the Potomac

Fort Sumter in Charleston harbor. Lincoln refused. On April 12, Confederate batteries bombarded Sumter, which surrendered the next day. War had begun. North and South called for thousands of volunteers. Each expected an easy victory over the other. The first major battle came that July, a Confederate triumph at Manassas Junction, Virginia.

Lincoln and the North did not give up. Fighting broke out in many places, with each side winning and losing small engagements. General George B. McClellan took charge of the Union Army. McClellan patiently equipped and trained his troops for a long and bloody struggle.

IRISH RECRUITING POSTER

DRILLING RECRUITS

Many graduates of the United States Military Academy at West Point led the opposing armies. They trained troops, designed fortifications, and organized supply departments. The volunteers of both sides had little time for training before they met at Bull Run (Manassas). Parts of the battle turned into confused mob scenes. Training then became more methodical. Officers and soldiers worked long hours until regiments learned to march and maneuver as disciplined units.

A THICKET OF BAYONETS
Union volunteers drill in their camp outside Washington, D.C. in the fall of 1861. General McClellan was determined to train his soldiers before sending them into action in a second invasion of Virginia.

UNION TROOPS ON PARADE
Mounted officers look on as troops march in step. The captain walks backward as his company takes up position.

August	September	October	November
Battle of Wilson's Creek, Missouri	Confederate troops enter Kentucky	Battle of Ball's Bluff, Virginia	Union Navy captures Port Royal, South Carolina
Fort Hatteras, North Carolina captured by Union	Siege of Lexington, Missouri		Confederate statesmen Mason and Slidell seized aboard British ship

FIRST GUNS AT SUMTER

Fort Sumter sat on an artificial island guarding Charleston harbor. The fort was under construction and unfinished. It was five-sided and made of brick, with walls 40 feet high and eight to twelve feet thick. In command was Major Robert Anderson, a Mexican War veteran and formerly a gunnery instructor at West Point.

Anderson had 84 officers and men, with 48 guns, but little ammunition or food. In December 1860, he had secretly moved his garrison to Sumter from a mainland fort. There, on its island, the fort was easier to defend if secessionists attacked. Anderson's move infuriated the Confederates, who called it an act of war. Their cannon were placed around the harbor, aiming at the fort. When a Union ship attempted to bring supplies to Sumter in January, Confederates drove it off with cannon fire.

By April, President Davis was determined to force Sumter's evacuation. He threatened bombardment when Anderson refused to surrender immediately. Then, at 4:30 AM on April 12, General P.G.T. Beauregard ordered Confederate guns to open fire. Anderson's garrison could make only a weak reply to the Confederate barrage. Thousands of Charleston residents gathered to watch the bombardment, which went on through the night.

On the second day, fires broke out in the fort, and Anderson had to give up. The bombardment had lasted 34 hours, but no one was killed, though 4,000 shells had struck Sumter. Then came the first death of a soldier on

IN THE HEAT OF BATTLE
Big guns roar inside the casemates of Fort Sumter on April 12, 1861, starting the Civil War. The fort was strong and its garrison courageous, but there was a severe shortage of ammunition and food.

Losses	
Union:	1 killed, 2 wounded
C.S.A.:	none

SOUTH
CAROLINA

CHARLESTON SULLIVAN'S
ISLAND
FT. SUMTER
JAMES
ISLAND

ATLANTIC OCEAN

A FORTIFIED HARBOR
Fort Sumter's guns dominated Charleston
harbor. Confederate batteries were on several
islands, including Sullivan's. A mortar on
James Island fired the first shot of the war.

April 14. Sumter's guns were firing a
salute as the flag was lowered, and
gunpowder accidentally exploded,
killing Private Daniel Hough.

The Civil War had begun. Private
Hough was its first fatality.

*Cast iron
cannonball*

C.S.A. CANNONBALL
One of many cannonballs
fired at Fort Sumter from Fort
Moultrie, on Sullivan's Island.

THE LEADERSHIP

MAJOR ANDERSON, OF KENTUCKY, commanded at Fort
Sumter. He had served in Indian conflicts and was
wounded in the Mexican War. General Beauregard,
from Louisiana, led C.S.A. forces. Beauregard had
also fought in the Mexican War. Both leaders
were West Point graduates.

> *"[The Confederacy will raise
> 100,000 men] to repel
> invasion...and to secure
> independence..."*
>
> —Davis, after the fall
> of Fort Sumter

JEFFERSON DAVIS (1808–1889)
President Davis, a native Kentuckian, was a West Pointer
and had served on the Northwest frontier and in the
Mexican War. He had been U.S. secretary of war and
a senator from Mississippi before secession.

> *"The government will not assail you. You
> can have no conflict without being
> yourselves the aggressors."*
>
> —Lincoln, in his inaugural address, March 1861

ABRAHAM LINCOLN (1809–1865)
Also a native Kentuckian, President Lincoln
was raised in Indiana and Illinois. His military
experience was volunteer militia service
during an Indian uprising in 1832.

REBELS WHIP McDOWELL

By early summer, politicians, journalists, and the Northern public wanted Lincoln to invade Virginia. They were sure of a quick victory if the army massing at Washington, D.C., marched against Richmond.

Union commanding general Winfield Scott knew his inexperienced troops were not ready. So did General Irvin McDowell, who was to lead them. McDowell wanted more time to train and equip the army, but pressure to invade mounted. One reason pushing the Union to act was that most of its troops had enlisted for only three months. By late July, they would be discharged, and the army would melt away.

McDowell moved out his 30,000 men on July 16, heading for Manassas, Virginia. There, he expected to engage the 20,000-man army under General Beauregard, victor at Fort Sumter. When McDowell advanced, a Confederate force of 9,500 men under General Joseph E. Johnston prepared to board trains for a 50-mile journey to Manassas. If Johnston

General's stars

BEAUREGARD'S EPAULETS
General Beauregard wore these brass epaulets. Fancy epaulets like these were part of a general's dress uniform and when not worn, were stored in a hard leather case.

RETAKING THE FLAG
Men of the 69th New York State Militia struggle to recapture their green flag, about to fall into hands of the advancing Confederates at the battle of First Bull Run.

Losses	
Union:	418 killed, 1,011 wounded, 1,216 missing
C.S.A.:	387 killed, 1,582 wounded, 12 missing

reached the battlefield in time, McDowell would lose the advantage.

On July 21, a hot and steamy Sunday, McDowell attacked and drove the C.S.A. forces back. Virginia troops, led by general Thomas J. Jackson, held position and stopped the Federals.

BEAUREGARD AND JOHNSTON   McDOWELL

Jackson won the name "Stonewall" for his stand that day. Then Johnston's reinforcements arrived, and Beauregard ordered a general assault. The Union army began to withdraw.

McDowell tried to reorganize his force, but many troops panicked and became a frightened mob, rushing back to Washington.

ARMIES COLLIDE
McDowell moved toward Manassas, and so did hundreds of civilians from Washington, eager to see the battle. When the Union was routed, the frightened civilians were caught up in the retreat.

THE LEADERSHIP

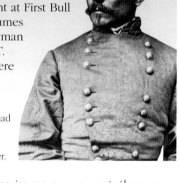

TOP CONFEDERATE GENERALS were present at First Bull Run: Jackson, Johnston, Jubal Early, James Longstreet, Richard Ewell, and cavalryman J.E.B. Stuart. Union colonels William T. Sherman and Ambrose E. Burnside were promoted to general after the battle.

PIERRE G.T. BEAUREGARD (1818-1893)
General Beauregard was a Louisiana native who had been fired as superintendent at West Point for supporting secession. He led at Bull Run, but Johnston was overall Confederate field commander.

"It was in no sense a civil war, but a war between two countries—for conquest on one side, for self-preservation on the other."

—Beauregard, writing after the war

IRVIN MCDOWELL (1818-1885)
A classmate of Beauregard at West Point, General McDowell was a career officer who was a tactics instructor at the Academy. His allies in the Lincoln government helped win him field command.

"We are not discouraged."

—General Winfield Scott, in a telegram to the defeated McDowell

STRUGGLE FOR MISSOURI

I n the summer of 1861, Union general Nathaniel Lyon drove Missouri's secessionist governor out of St. Louis and organized a fighting force. Lyon

> *"Our ammunition was exhausted, our men undisciplined, and we feared to risk pursuit."*
>
> —Nicholas B. Pearce, Confederate general at Wilson's Creek

AN EARLY BATTLE
Missouri hung in the balance as General Lyon led his Union army against rebels camped near Springfield, the state capital.

had fewer than 6,000 men, but in August he boldly marched out to defeat a Confederate army of 12,000, under General Sterling Price.

Lyon surprised Price's camp near Wilson's Creek on August 10. At first, the rebels were driven back, but Lyon

was killed. The Confederates counterattacked and a fierce battle surged back and forth. Finally, the exhausted armies broke off the fighting, and the Federals retreated.

Price went on to capture Springfield, the state capital.

THE LEADERSHIP

PRICE UNITED WITH TENNESSEE GENERAL Ben McCullouch to lead the Confederate forces at Wilson's Creek. General Nathaniel Lyon, from Connecticut, was a West Pointer with Mexican War experience.

STERLING PRICE (1809–1867)
Commander of the Missouri State Guard before the war, Price had been a congressman and governor of his native Missouri. A general in the Mexican War, Price recruited and trained thousands of pro-Confederate volunteers from Missouri.

THE FALL OF LYON
One of the North's first military heroes, the fiery Lyon was wounded three times at Wilson's Creek, the last time fatally.

Losses

Union: 223 killed, 721 wounded, 291 missing

C.S.A.: 257 killed, 900 wounded, 27 missing

A NAVAL TRIUMPH

The industrial North rapidly built up a strong fleet of warships and gunboats. This gave the Union control of the South's coastal waters.

In October, Federal forces set out to establish a new base of naval operations by capturing Port Royal, South Carolina. The 17-vessel fleet of Admiral Samuel F. Du Pont transported 12,000 soldiers into Port Royal Sound. The troops were led by General Thomas W. Sherman.

On November 7, Du Pont's warships bombarded Forts Beauregard and Walker, guarding the sound. The defenders were unable to withstand the cannonade and had to evacuate. Soon afterward, an overwhelming force of Federals landed on the shore and took possession of the empty forts.

The naval operations in Port Royal Sound were known as the Hilton Head campaign.

STRATEGIC PORT
Port Royal became a Union naval base for operations against South Carolina, Georgia, and Florida.

THE LEADERSHIP

GENERAL THOMAS SHERMAN, a West Point graduate, served with distinction throughout the war. Sherman lost a leg in 1863, but stayed in the army.

"A superior naval force must command the whole . . . of the coast."

—Du Pont report to the Navy Department, July 1861

SAMUEL F. DU PONT (1803–1865)
Admiral Du Pont was in charge of the Philadelphia Navy Yard in 1860. A New Jerseyan, Du Pont was president of a Federal board that planned naval operations.

Losses	
Union:	31 killed/wounded/missing
C.S.A.:	66 killed/wounded/missing

A NAVAL ASSAULT
Confederate shells fall short of a Federal warship bombarding Port Royal forts.

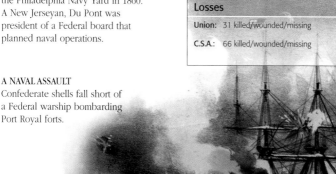

The War in the South Intensifies

Federal armies began to conquer the Mississippi Valley, fighting their way downriver. Gunboat fleets helped capture river forts, and the Confederates were forced to fall back.

In the spring, C.S.A. general Albert Johnston surprised Ulysses Grant at Pittsburg Landing, Tennessee. Grant held the field in the bloodiest battle yet, called Shiloh.

Flag Officer David Farragut captured New Orleans, and other river towns surrendered. Only Port Hudson, Louisiana, and Vicksburg, Mississippi, held out.

Meanwhile, McClellan invaded Virginia's Peninsula region and advanced toward Richmond. Confederate commander Joseph Johnston was wounded. He was replaced by Robert E. Lee, military advisor to President Davis. Lee defeated McClellan and drove the Union off the Peninsula.

In July, Lincoln called for 300,000 three-year enlistments to build an army

UNDER THE GUNS
Union warships battle past forts defending the Mississippi near New Orleans. The cannonade was described like all the world's earthquakes, thunder, and lightning exploding at once.

George McClellan

February	March	April	May
Grant captures Fort Henry and Fort Donelson, in Tennessee	Battle of Pea Ridge, Arkansas	McClellan begins siege of Yorktown, Virginia	Jackson begins his Shenandoah Valley Campaign
	USS *Monitor* fights CSS *Virginia* at Hampton Roads, Virginia	Battle of Shiloh, Tennessee	Battle of Fair Oaks (Seven Pines), Virginia begins
		Fall of New Orleans	

for a long war. John Pope replaced McClellan and blundered his way to a second Union defeat at Bull Run in August. Lee invaded Maryland, and McClellan was brought back. In September, he stopped Lee at Antietam Creek.

Now Lincoln reinforced the Union cause by declaring slaves in rebellious states were free.

When McClellan did not aggressively pursue Lee after Antietam, Lincoln replaced him with Ambrose E. Burnside. General Burnside admitted to not knowing how to lead a large army. That December, thousands of Union soldiers were slaughtered at Fredericksburg, proving he was right.

EMANCIPATION PROCLAMATION

"FOREVER FREE"

Lincoln worried the British government might recognize the C.S.A, but knew the British people were antislavery. If the Union abolished slavery, Britain would not be able to support the South. Though few Northerners wanted a war just to abolish slavery, most agreed with the Emancipation Proclamation, which declared the South's 3.5 million slaves "thenceforward and forever, free."

A SLAVE FAMILY
Five generations of African-Americans are pictured on a South Carolina plantation. The Emancipation Proclamation would free them only if the North won the war.

AFTER ANTIETAM
President Lincoln poses with General McClellan and his staff officers after the Battle of Antietam, in the fall of 1862.

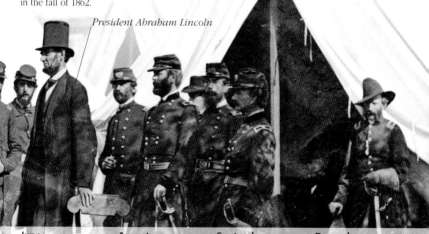

President Abraham Lincoln

June	August	September	December
Seven Days' Battles begin in Virginia	Second Bull Run (Second Manassas), Virginia	Fall of Harpers Ferry, West Virginia	Battle of Fredericksburg, Virginia
		Battle of Antietam, Maryland	Battle of Stones River (Murfreesboro), Tennessee begins
		Emancipation Proclamation	

GUNBOATS IN TENNESSEE

Confederate forts in the western theater blocked Union advances. On the Cumberland River in Tennessee stood Fort Donelson. Fort Henry was on the Tennessee River. In early February, Union flag officer

> *"There was so much blood on [the decks] that our men could not work the guns without slipping."*
>
> —Union officer at Donelson bombardment

Andrew H. Foote's gunboat fleet cooperated with General Ulysses S. Grant's army to attack the forts.

The Union vessels included four ironclads, each with 12 guns. Henry was weakly defended and surrendered after a brief bombardment. Donelson had 15,000 troops and required a siege. Foote was wounded in an artillery exchange with C.S.A. batteries. The Confederates attempted to break out, but failed. They surrendered to Grant on February 16.

▬▬▬ FOOTE AND GRANT

STRATEGIC RIVERS
Kentucky and Tennessee could be controlled from the Cumberland and Tenneseee rivers, where Confederate forts Donelson and Henry defended the passages.

THE LEADERSHIP

GRANT'S VICTORY MADE HIM FAMOUS in the North, which desperately needed good news. C.S.A. general Simon Buckner, a West Pointer, surrendered Fort Donelson to Grant. He was exchanged and fought to the end of the war.

ANDREW H. FOOTE (1806–1863)
Foote took charge of the western flotilla at the start of the war. Congress promoted him to rear admiral after Fort Donelson, but his wound did not heal. He died in 1863, while on his way to assume naval command off Charleston.

Losses Forts Henry and Donelson	
Union:	511 killed, 2,139 wounded, 229 missing
C.S.A.:	2,000 killed/wounded, 14,686 missing

A GUNBOAT BARRAGE
Union ironclad gunboats steam close together on the Tennessee River as they bombard Fort Henry, which soon fell.

DARING PLANS FAIL

Confederate forces withdrew from Missouri and reorganized in Arkansas, where General Earl Van Dorn took command. He decided to go after the 11,000-man army of General Samuel R. Curtis.

> *"[I plan] attempting St. Louis and carrying the war into Illinois."*
>
> —Van Dorn on his bold plan to capture St. Louis and invade the North

They met at Pea Ridge, Arkansas, on March 7. Van Dorn had about 17,000 men, including three regiments of Indian volunteers. Van Dorn sent a risky assault against the enemy rear, but Curtis blocked the maneuver.

COMING TO GRIPS
Union troops under Samuel Curtis and the Confederates of Earl Van Dorn maneuvered toward a decisive Union victory.

▇▇▇ VAN DORN
▇▇▇ CURTIS

Key C.S.A. officers were killed in Van Dorn's attack and the Federal counterattack. The next day, Federal assaults drove him from the field. The Union now had a strong grip on Missouri. Van Dorn was ordered to join the Mississippi River forces.

THE LEADERSHIP

GENERAL CURTIS RESIGNED AS AN IOWA congressman to serve the Union. A West Point graduate, he had Mexican War experience. His subordinate, General Franz Sigel, went on to fight against Stonewall Jackson in the east.

EARL VAN DORN (1820–1863)
A West Pointer, General Van Dorn was a veteran of the Mexican and Indian wars. He was in charge of all Mississippi troops and later was a cavalry leader. He was murdered by a jealous husband in 1863.

Losses	
Union:	1,384 killed/wounded/missing
C.S.A.:	800 killed/wounded/missing

PREPARED TO FIRE
Union cannoneers take aim at charging Confederate cavalry in the Battle of Pea Ridge.

25

CLASH OF IRONCLADS

At the start of hostilities, Federals abandoned and burned the navy yard at Norfolk, Virginia. They destroyed the steamer *Merrimack,* then under repair. The Confederates converted her hull into the "ironclad" ram *Virginia.* She was 170 feet long, with sloping sides protected by four-inch iron bars. She carried six nine-inch cannons and four rifled guns.

The Union ironclad *Monitor* was a special design, while the *Virginia* was built with the materials at hand. The *Monitor* had two 11-inch cannon in a

circular turret covered by thick iron plates. She was much more manageable than the *Virginia,* but her shape looked like a "cheesebox on a raft."

On March 8, *Virginia* attacked the Federal fleet at Hampton Roads. She rammed and sank the wooden-hulled frigate *Cumberland* and captured the 50-gun *Congress.* The *Virginia* seemed invincible, with the power to destroy or drive off the entire Union fleet. The *Monitor* appeared the next day, and a duel of ironclads began.

The *Monitor* and *Virginia* actually

THE LEADERSHIP

C.S.A. CAPTAIN AND *VIRGINIA* COMMANDER, Franklin Buchanan, was the first superintendent of the U.S. Naval Academy and had been in China expeditions. Wounded while commanding the *Virginia,* he later was promoted to C.S.A. admiral.

"We of the Monitor *thought, and still think, that we gained a great victory."*

—Commander S. Dana Greene, who took over the *Monitor* after Worden was injured

JOHN L. WORDEN (1818–1897)
Commander Worden supervised the construction of the *Monitor.* He was a career naval officer before the Civil War. During the battle with the ironclad *Virginia,* Worden was temporarily blinded by an explosion. He retired in 1886 as a rear admiral.

"[The Virginia *is] exceedingly difficult to work."*

—Report of commander Catesby Jones, whose vessel took on the *Monitor*

CATESBY JONES (1821–1877)
Lieutenant Jones supervised the arming of the *Virginia.* He took over command from Admiral Franklin Buchanan, who was wounded during the *Virginia's* attack on Union warships. Jones fought the *Monitor* to a draw.

touched sides, but their guns could not penetrate each other. The three-hour battle ended with little damage to either vessel. Neither ship did much else afterward. The *Virginia* was scuttled that March when the Confederates abandoned Norfolk navy yards. In December, the *Monitor* sank in heavy seas off Cape Hatteras.

Both sides constructed new ironclads along the lines of these vessels. Navy men were astonished by how even heavily armed wooden-hulled warships were useless against them. Around the world, navies raced to build their own ironclads. After Hampton Roads, fighting ships would never be the same.

STRATEGIC RIVERS
Early in the war, Federal naval power won control of the Hampton Roads waterway, which led into the heart of Virginia. Here, the *Monitor* neutralized the C.S.A. ironclad *Virginia*.

SMOKE AND FLAMES
Try as they would, the ironclads *Monitor* and *Virginia* could not dent each other at Hampton Roads, Virginia, in March 1862. Naval warfare changed forever, as other nations studied the construction of ironclads and built their own models.

FLATTENED CANNONBALL
This solid iron cannonball was fired at the CSS *Virginia*, formerly the *Merrimack*, and flattened when it struck the ship's iron siding.

Losses: Land and Naval	
Union:	409 killed/wounded/missing
C.S.A.:	21 killed/wounded/missing

BLOODY SHILOH

On April 6, the Federal camp along the Tennessee River near Pittsburg Landing awoke to a mild spring morning. Ulysses Grant's 37,000 troops ate their Sunday breakfast, unworried about the enemy. Albert S. Johnston's Confederate army was thought to be 25 miles away in Mississippi. Grant would move against him soon.

Grant and his staff had not thought it necessary to dig entrenchments to protect the camp. One of his generals, William T. Sherman, even scoffed at reports of Confederate activity not far from his own camp at Shiloh Church.

At 6 AM, the woods near Sherman erupted with firing. The startled Union forces grabbed for their weapons as thousands of Confederates attacked.

The Federals were sent reeling. Johnston had made a rapid march and concealed his troops in the woods until daybreak. It seemed the Federals would be driven back to the river.

Grant was everywhere at once, rallying his men. A battle line under General Benjamin M. Prentiss refused to retreat. They held a fearful front that would be called the "Hornet's Nest" because of all the bullets buzzing in the air. Prentiss and 2,200 survivors finally had to surrender, but they had

RALLYING HIS TROOPS
Battle-weary Confederate soldiers salute General Albert Sydney Johnston during the struggle at Shiloh in Tennessee. Soon after, Johnston was shot in the leg and died from loss of blood.

Losses	
Union:	1,754 killed, 8,408 wounded, 2,885 missing
C.S.A.:	1,723 killed, 8,012 wounded, 959 missing

saved the day. Grant's army was recovering and forming battle lines. Cannon blasted at close range, and the roar of conflict was deafening. The Federals turned back charge after charge. In mid-afternoon, Johnston was killed, and General Beauregard took command.

That night, Grant received 25,000 reinforcements. The next day he went on the attack, and the outnumbered Beauregard withdrew southward. Both sides claimed victory, but the Union now held the advantage in the western theater.

JOHNSTON'S UNEXPECTED ATTACK
Grant and Johnston's armies were about equal in size. Knowing Grant would soon be reinforced, Johnston advanced from Corinth to attack Grant's camp first.

JOHNSTON   GRANT

At Shiloh, Grant was taught a bitter lesson. By underestimating the enemy, he had nearly been defeated. He would not do so again.

THE LEADERSHIP

GRANT'S DIVISION COMMANDERS included Mexican War veterans Benjamin M. Prentiss and Lew Wallace. Beauregard was Confederate second-in-command; West Pointers William Hardee, Braxton Bragg, and Leonidas Polk were corps commanders.

ULYSSES S. GRANT (1822-1885)
An undistinguished West Point cadet, Grant won honors for gallantry in the Mexican War. He left the army in 1854, returning in 1861 to command in southern Illinois. Victory at Shiloh brought him fame, although he was faulted for being unprepared for the enemy attack.

"Better troops never went upon a battlefield..."
—Grant describes his army after Shiloh

ALBERT SYDNEY JOHNSTON (1803-1862)
A Kentuckian and a West Pointer, Johnston commanded troops in the Republic of Texas army that fought Mexico. He rejoined the U.S. Army and rose to general. In 1861, he turned down the rank of second-in-command of the Union Army to become a Confederate general.

"I would fight them if they were a million."
—Johnston, aware reinforcements are coming to Grant

CRESCENT CITY CAPTURED

The Civil War's western theater included the mid-Mississippi River Valley and its tributary rivers. Union possession of the Mississippi would cut the Confederacy in two. Texas, Louisiana, and Arkansas would be unable to send men and supplies eastward to aid the war effort. First, Union forces had to capture New Orleans near the river's mouth.

Though she was the South's greatest city, the Confederacy had done little to protect the "Crescent City." Forts Jackson and St. Philips guarded the passage from the Gulf of Mexico, but few troops were available to commanding general Mansfield Lovell. Local commanders were furious that the C.S.A. government at Richmond was slow to strengthen New Orleans.

Lovell could not prevent 15,000 Union troops landing on several coastal islands by March. This force was commanded by General Benjamin Butler. The Union plan was for Butler to move on New Orleans after the river forts were taken.

In April, Union naval commander David Farragut led 24 warships and 19 mortar boats against the forts. His mortars fired 17,000 rounds in a week-long bombardment, but with little result. Farragut

Stars represent Confederate states

CONFEDERATE PENNANT
This Confederate naval pennant flew on the gunboat CSS *McRae* which fought against Farragut's fleet near Forts Jackson and St. Philip. CSS *McRae* was badly damaged in the engagement and her commander mortally wounded.

USELESS GUNFIRE
This Union warship's cannons cannot fend off a rushing ram that drove a hole in the ship's side, but did not sink her. Farragut's fleet forced its way upstream to capture New Orleans.

Losses	
Union:	36 killed, 135 wounded
C.S.A.:	50 killed/wounded

decided to dash past the forts and directly attack the undefended city.

At 2 AM on April 24, the Union fleet steamed upriver, flags flying, guns blazing. They came under a hurricane of enemy fire, but rushed past the forts with little damage. Lovell's tiny C.S.A. fleet of gunboats and beak-prowed rams made a brave counterattack that was wiped out. Lovell's own vessel narrowly escaped. Farragut lost only one ship, sunk by a Confederate ram.

On April 25, the New Orleans civil authorities surrendered to avoid a bombardment by Farragut's fleet.

FARRAGUT'S ROUTE UP THE MISSISSIPPI

UNION WARSHIPS TRIUMPH

Forts St. Philips and Jackson blocked the Mississippi passage to New Orleans 90 miles upstream. Farragut rushed past their guns instead of engaging in artillery duels.

THE LEADERSHIP

COMMANDER DAVID D. PORTER, Farragut's foster brother, led the mortar boat fleet. Union general Benjamin Butler occupied New Orleans. C.S.A. captain Beverley Kennon, commanding a ram, fought gallantly and was captured.

DAVID G. FARRAGUT (1801–1870)

In the navy since the age of nine, Farragut served through the War of 1812 and saw action in the Mexican War. He had been living at the naval base in Norfolk, Virginia, when the Civil War began.

"Conquer or be conquered."

—Farragut to his officers
before running the guns

MANSFIELD LOVELL (1822–1884)

Lovell had been an artillery student at West Point and was a Mexican War veteran. He worked as a street commissioner for New York City until the Civil War. Headquartered at New Orleans, he commanded several small river forts.

"[New Orleans was lost because of] the stupidity, tardiness, ignorance, and neglect of the authorities in Richmond."

—Captain Beverley Kennon, C.S.A. Navy, commander of
the ram *Governor Moore*

31

JACKSON STRIKES HARD

In April, McClellan advanced toward Richmond from the Virginia Peninsula. He counted on reinforcements from forces operating in or near the Shenandoah Valley. C.S.A. general Thomas ("Stonewall") Jackson was ordered to keep these reinforcements from him.

Jackson marched fast and struck hard in the Shenandoah. At first, he had only 4,200 men, facing ten times more troops under generals Nathaniel Banks, John Frémont, and Robert Milroy. The Union forces had, however, no overall commander to coordinate their efforts. Early in May, Jackson defeated Milroy in the southerly hills. He then hurried northward, traveling a remarkable 35 miles a day as his men earned the name "Jackson's foot cavalry." He was reinforced to 17,000 and proceeded to defeat Federal forces before they could combine to outnumber him. Banks lost at Winchester, and Frémont at Cross Keys.

Lincoln and Secretary of War Edwin Stanton thought Jackson was a threat to Washington. So they withheld the reinforcements McClellan needed. The generals in the Shenandoah planned with Irvin McDowell's army to trap Jackson. More than 50,000 troops converged on him, but his hard-driving army slipped through the net.

By June, Jackson had thrown Union forces in the Shenandoah into disarray, keeping them from going to McClellan's aid. Next, Jackson hurried away to support Lee against McClellan.

A CHEER FROM THE "FOOT CAVALRY"
Stonewall Jackson is saluted by his men during the 1862 Shenandoah Valley Campaign. Jackson wore a weathered cadet cap that was described as "pulled so low in front that the visor cut the glint of his eyeballs."

Losses

Union: approximately 3,600 killed/
       wounded/missing

C.S.A.: approximately 1,600 killed/
       wounded/missing

It is said that the U.S. government's fear of Jackson caused the war to drag on three more years. If McClellan had been reinforced with the full might of the Union armies, Richmond surely would have fallen. Instead, Stonewall Jackson and his "foot cavalry" earned a reputation as being unbeatable in battle.

C.S.A. DRUM CANTEEN
Drum-style canteens were cheap to manufacture and were widely used by the South. Sometimes covered with cloth, they had linen or leather slings.

Canteen made from tin

JACKSON'S ROUTE

JACKSON'S CAMPAIGN
Stonewall Jackson led his army through the Shenandoah Valley, defeating Union forces at Winchester, New Market, Cross Keys, Front Royal, and McDowell.

THE LEADERSHIP

JACKSON HAD EXCELLENT GENERALS in Richard Ewell, also a West Pointer, and cavalryman Turner Ashby, killed in the campaign. Union leaders ranged from the incompetent Banks to the brilliant Colonel George H. Gordon, a West Pointer.

JOHN C. FRÉMONT (1813–1880)
Frémont had been an explorer, California's governor and senator, and had run for president as a Republican in 1856. Though unsuccessful commanding in the West, Frémont took charge of troops opposing Jackson. In mid-1862, Frémont was relieved of command.

"It was too late to remedy the ill effects of the division of commands...."
—Union general Jacob D. Cox, describing Jackson's escape

THOMAS J. JACKSON (1824–1863)
A Virginian and a West Pointer, Jackson was a Mexican War veteran. He was extremely devout. Jackson was considered Lee's right arm in major campaigns. He was accidentally killed by his own troops at the Battle of Chancellorsville in 1863.

"Always mystify, mislead, and surprise the enemy if possible; and when you strike and overcome him, never let up in the pursuit."
—Stonewall Jackson

JOHNSTON BLOCKS McCLELLAN

A fter landing on the Peninsula in March, Union forces advanced to within six miles of Richmond by April. McClellan's army numbered 112,000, facing 60,000 C.S.A. troops under Joseph E. Johnston.

Johnston saw a chance to destroy the corps of Erasmus Keyes, isolated south of the Chickahominy River. Most of the Union army was north of the river, which was flooded and difficult to cross. Keyes occupied Fair Oaks and Seven Pines, surrounded by wooded and swampy terrain.

Johnston ordered a dawn attack on May 31, but some of his units became mixed up on the narrow roads. This caused delays in moving troops forward. The battle did not begin until midday, and then only Daniel H. Hill's division launched an assault. Keyes recovered from the first attack, even counterattacking with bayonet charges. The main Confederate forces finally came into

the action and fought in heavy rain. McClellan ordered Edwin Sumner's corps to cross the swollen river and support Keyes. Sumner's troops slogged over muddy roads to join the battle, which became a standoff.

Johnston assumed personal command of the engagement at Fair

OBSERVATION BALLOON
Aerial reconnaissance was first used in the Civil War. This tethered hot-air balloon, named "Intrepid," carried observers high above the battlefield at Fair Oaks.

RESCUING THE COLORS
A standard bearer for the 104th Pennsylvania catches up his regiment's falling battle flag during a bayonet charge at Fair Oaks, Virginia.

Losses	
Union:	5,031 killed/wounded/missing
C.S.A.:	6,134 killed/wounded/missing

Oaks. He was wounded, and General Gustavus Smith took charge. Smith ordered renewed attacks the following day. Union reinforcements helped fight off the assaults. That afternoon, Robert E. Lee arrived to take command. He withdrew the C.S.A. army to its original defensive positions.

Despite the Federal advantage in total numbers, the forces actually engaged at Fair Oaks were about equal at 42,000 men each.

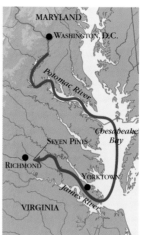

THE VIRGINIA PENINSULA
McClellan's army landed on the eastern peninsula formed by the York and James rivers. C.S.A. defenders fought a month-long delaying action before withdrawing to Richmond.

▬▬▬ McClellan

THE LEADERSHIP

PROMINENT UNION GENERALS were Sumner's divisional commander John Sedgwick and the corps commander Erasmus Keyes. Important C.S.A. leaders were Daniel H. Hill and Gustavus W. Smith, in charge of the left wing. All were West Pointers.

EDWIN SUMNER (1797-1863)
General Sumner was an army officer commanding in the West in 1861. He rose to command a corps in the Peninsular Campaign. He later took part in the Antietam and Fredericksburg campaigns. Falling ill, he died early in 1863.

"Impossible? Sir, I tell you I can cross! I am ordered!"

—Sumner, after being told a bridge over the Chickahominy was unsafe

"The shot that struck me down is the very best that has been fired for the Southern cause yet."

—Johnston, glad that Lee is the army's commander

JOSEPH E. JOHNSTON (1807-1891)
West Pointer Johnston resigned a generalship in the U.S. Army to accept a commission for the C.S.A. Johnston had won battlefield honors in the Mexican War. Though he feuded with President Davis, he served until the end of the war.

AT RICHMOND'S GATES

After Fair Oaks, Lee decided to strike McClellan, who was about to move on Richmond. The government in Washington eagerly expected a full-scale siege to begin.

Lee sent cavalry general J.E.B. Stuart to scout the Union positions. Stuart daringly rode right around the enemy. He told Lee that McClellan's right wing was vulnerable to attack. There, Fitz-John Porter's troops were north of the Chickahominy, while McClellan's main force was south of the river. On June 26, C.S.A. general Ambrose P. Hill began the attack on Porter, who repulsed the assaults. After the day's battle, known as Mechanicsville, McClellan ordered Porter's retreat to Gaines's Mill. The next day, Porter held out against superior attacking forces. He withdrew across the Chickahominy that night.

McClellan's supply line was threatened, and he began to withdraw his entire army. Seeing this, Lee attacked the following day near

THE LEADERSHIP

FITZ-JOHN PORTER FOUGHT HARD, handling his outnumbered troops skillfully. Lee's top generals were A.P. Hill, John Hood, D.H. Hill, James Longstreet, and Richard Ewell. They became pillars of Lee's army.

GEORGE B. MCCLELLAN (1826–1885)
As commander-in-chief, McClellan proved an excellent administrator as he built the Union army. A West Pointer, he was a decorated Mexican War veteran. He ran for president against Lincoln in 1864 and later was governor of New Jersey.

"I shall do my best to save the army. Send more gunboats."

—McClellan to government officials from Malvern Hill

ROBERT E. LEE (1807–1870)
Lee was a top cadet at West Point and later was the academy's superintendent. He made a reputation in the Mexican War and became a career officer. He turned down command of the Union armies and offered his services to Virginia. Lee is considered one of history's greatest generals.

"We sleep on the field and shall renew the contest in the morning."

—Lee's report to President Davis after Gaines's Mill

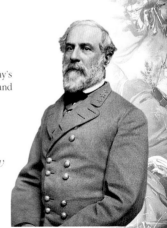

Savage's Station. As the main Union army withdrew, Lee struck its rear guard at White Oak Swamp. With each assault, the Southerners were repulsed. On July 1, more frontal attacks at Malvern Hill cost Lee heavily. The Federal cannoneers performed superbly. Union artillery was becoming far superior to C.S.A. artillery.

Though his army had beaten back Lee's attacks in these seven days, McClellan withdrew to the James River. McClellan no longer threatened Richmond, and Lincoln was dismayed.

McClellan offered a new offensive plan, but Lincoln was disgusted with him. He ordered McClellan to send his troops to General John Pope, who was in northern Virginia. McClellan was left without a command.

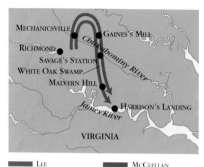

▬▬ LEE   ▬▬ McCLELLAN

PATH OF RETREAT
Lee attacked and attacked again, as McClellan made a fighting withdrawal from his position in front of Richmond. Seven days of battles, June 26 to July 2, resulted in McClellan's army leaving the Peninsula.

RED DEVILS
The 5th New York Volunteers wore colorful uniforms styled on the Zouaves, native troops with the French in North Africa. Under heavy fire in the battle of Gaines's Mill, a sergeant plants the regimental flag in front of the battle line and defies the Confederates.

Losses
Union: 15,849 killed/wounded/missing

C.S.A.: 20,733 killed/wounded/missing

A UNION ARMY SMASHED

Early in August, Jackson was again in the Shenandoah Valley. This time his opponent was Nathaniel Banks. They met at Cedar Mountain. Banks was driving Jackson back when A.P. Hill arrived just in time to counterattack and win the battle. Next Lee had to decide what to do with the powerful force John Pope was gathering in northern Virginia.

In mid-August, Lee learned that strong reinforcements from McClellan's army were on their way to Pope. In five days, Pope's army would double to 130,000. Lee decided to attack immediately. He called for Jackson to join him, and on August 25 the campaign was on.

Jackson's 20,000 men and Stuart's cavalry marched more than 60 miles in two days and destroyed Pope's supply depot at Manassas. Pope's 62,000 troops attacked Jackson on August 29. This brought on the larger battle, as Lee's main army, led by Longstreet, arrived.

Sergeant's stripes

UNION SERGEANT'S JACKET
Worn by a sergeant in the 27th New York Volunteers, this short jacket is trimmed in blue and has an exterior breast pocket.

THE DIEHARDS
Men of a Louisiana brigade, out of ammunition, stubbornly refuse to retreat. They hurl rocks to hold off a Union charge. Confederate reinforcements arrived in time to repulse the enemy attack.

Losses
Union: 1,724 killed, 8,372 wounded, 5,958 missing

C.S.A.: 1,481 killed, 7,627 wounded, 89 missing

Their force was 50,000. The Confederate left wing repelled relentless attacks led by General Philip Kearny. The next day, Pope again attacked Lee's left, but was repulsed each time. Then Lee's right wing, under Longstreet, attacked Pope's left and drove him across Bull Run,

beaten. Kearny was killed later in the campaign, while fighting off further C.S.A. attacks. Pope pulled the Union army back to the safety of Washington's defenses.

The Union had more than 16,000 casualties, the C.S.A. more than 9,000. Lee had repulsed the siege of Richmond and defeated Pope. Southern commanders seemed superior to what the North had to offer.

LEE   POPE

RETREAT TO WASHINGTON
John Pope expected to command a massive Union army. Those hopes were dashed when Lee defeated him at Manassas Junction and drove him back to Washington.

THE LEADERSHIP

UNION GENERAL PHILIP KEARNY distinguished himself on the Peninsula and at Second Bull Run. He was killed when he rode accidentally into C.S.A. lines. "Jeb" Stuart's cavalry made a daring raid on Pope's headquarters.

JAMES LONGSTREET (1821-1904)
Known as Lee's "Old War Horse," Longstreet was a dependable subordinate commander. A West Pointer and Mexican War veteran, Longstreet served in Lee's campaigns to the end of the war, in spite of a serious wound.

"General Lee urged me to go in, and of course I was anxious to meet his wishes."

—Longstreet's memoir of his attack at Second Bull Run

JOHN POPE (1822-1892)
A West Pointer who served in the Mexican War, Pope was a topographical engineer when the Civil War began. Successful in the mid-Mississippi region, he was brought east to command an army in northern Virginia.

"In the saddle."

—Pope's reply to reporters who asked where his headquarters would be

McCLELLAN REPULSES LEE

After Second Bull Run, Lee invaded Maryland, Lincoln fired Pope, and McClellan resumed command. Lee sent Jackson against Harpers Ferry, and Longstreet's force went northward. The Army of Northern Virginia was ragged, many of the men went barefoot. Yet it had the fighting spirit of "hungry wolves," an observer said.

Small battles developed, and Lee decided to pull his army together before McClellan attacked. Lee had about 40,000 men, McClellan twice as many. On September 15, Harpers Ferry fell to Jackson, who then rushed to join Lee at Sharpsburg.

By September 16, Lee was prepared. On September 17, the Federals assaulted Lee's left, then his center. A third assault was to come on Lee's right, over Antietam Creek on a stone bridge. Here, Federal commander Ambrose Burnside was slow in getting started. Lee's left and center held against the attacks of John Mansfield, Joseph Hooker, and Sumner. Burnside finally fought his way across the bridge, and Lee's right was driven back. At the last moment, A.P. Hill's division completed a grueling march from Harpers Ferry. Hill counterattacked and saved Lee's right wing.

The fighting broke off, ending in a draw. September 17 would be the bloodiest day of the Civil War. Union casualties numbered more than 12,000;

LONE STAR AT ANTIETAM
A standard bearer of the First Texas regiment waves his state's Lone Star flag while fighting in a cornfield. The regiment became isolated and suffered more than 80 percent casualties and the loss of their flags.

Losses	
Union:	2,108 killed, 9,549 wounded, 753 missing
C.S.A.:	2,700 killed, 9,024 wounded, 2,000 missing

the C.S.A. almost 14,000. Neither army renewed the attack. On the night of September 18, Lee withdrew toward Virginia. Lincoln urged McClellan to follow and attack Lee immediately. When McClellan did not, he was again removed from command.

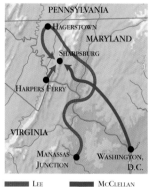

A ZOUAVE FEZ

Several regiments had uniforms like French-Moroccan "Zouave" soldiers. This fez is from the 9th New York Regiment (Hawkins' Zouaves), which was at Antietam.

ANTIETAM

Lee's forces moved north, and McClellan kept between them and Washington. He and Lee engaged at Antietam Creek, near Sharpsburg, Maryland.

THE LEADERSHIP

A.P. HILL HAD BECOME ONE OF LEE'S finest generals, a man who often saved the day. "Up came Hill!" was part of several C.S.A. battle reports. Union generals Burnside and Hooker were noticed, and Lincoln named Burnside to replace McClellan.

AMBROSE P. HILL (1825–1865)

Hill was a West Pointer who served in the Mexican and Seminole wars. His troops were known for their speed in marching. He fought as a corps commander until the 1865 Petersburg campaign, when he was killed.

"At the last moment, A.P. Hill came in to reinforce him. . . ."

—Longstreet recalls a crucial moment at Antietam

JOSEPH K.F. MANSFIELD (1803–1862)

Mansfield was a Mexican War veteran and a West Pointer. He superintended Southern coastal defenses. At almost 60 years of age, Mansfield served in the Peninsular Campaign and died leading his corps at Antietam.

"Yes, yes, you are right."

—Mansfield's last words, agreeing that troops close by were the enemy

INTO A WALL OF FLAME

In mid-November, Burnside led his Army of the Potomac to the Rappahannock River across from Fredericksburg, Virginia. Lee's army was off to the west, so Burnside could have broken through and rushed on Richmond. A rainstorm flooded the river, however, causing delay. Lee hurried back to fortify the town.

Burnside's engineers built pontoon bridges under deadly enemy fire. On December 13, his army crossed over to make a frontal assault. He had more than 116,000 troops against Lee's 72,000, but the Southerners were strongly entrenched on high ground.

As the enormous Union left wing began to advance, John Pelham's horse artillery galloped out in front of C.S.A. lines and opened fire. Pelham kept firing until Jeb Stuart recalled him, saying: "You infernal, gallant fool!" The Federals, too, were gallant that day. Regiment after regiment surged up the slopes into withering fire from defenders behind stone walls.

There were near breakthroughs, but Burnside's attack was suicidal. The

THE LEADERSHIP

JACKSON AND LONGSTREET COMMANDED LEE'S CORPS; generals Jubal Early and William Taliaferro led key counterattacks. Union division commander George Meade made a charge that almost broke through, but lacked reinforcements.

JOHN PELHAM (1838-1863)

Pelham resigned from West Point to fight for his home state, Alabama. A major in command of horse artillery—cannon that were pulled into action by horses—he developed skillful new tactics for this fast-moving weapon. He was killed at Kelly's Ford in 1863.

"It is glorious to see such courage in one so young."

—R.E. Lee, about Pelham's performance at Fredericksburg

AMBROSE E. BURNSIDE (1824-1881)

Inventor of a breech-loading rifle, Burnside was a West Pointer. He commanded a brigade at First Bull Run and later a coastal expedition. Burnside was finally relieved of command in 1864 for poorly handling troops.

"Oh those men! Those men over there! I am thinking of them all the time."

—Burnside, as the battle raged

slopes were covered with blue-jacketed dead. Union soldiers took cover from heavy fire by lying behind stacked up bodies of fallen men. More than 106,000 Federals were in the day-long attacks. Almost 13,000 were casualties; Lee suffered 5,300.

The next day, Burnside intended to renew the assault, but his generals talked him out of it. The battered Federals withdrew under darkness. Burnside was replaced by Joseph Hooker.

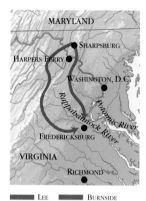

MARYLAND

SHARPSBURG

HARPERS FERRY

WASHINGTON, D.C.

Rappahannock River

Potomac River

FREDERICKSBURG

VIRGINIA

RICHMOND

■ LEE   ■ BURNSIDE

LEE ALMOST OUTMANEUVERED
Burnside surprised Lee by moving directly southward. Lee had expected him to defend Washington. Lee raced south just in time to fortify Fredericksburg. Burnside waited for his pontoon bridges to be built so he could cross the Rappahannock River.

Irish harp

IRISH REGIMENTAL FLAG
Symbols of a heritage, harps and shamrocks decorated the flags of the Union's Irish regiments. These were made up of Irish immigrants and Irish-Americans.

ASSAULTING MARYE'S HEIGHTS
Men of the Irish Brigade of the Union army follow their green battle flag into a storm of fire from Marye's Heights. They cry "Faugh-a-ballagh!"—"Clear the Way!" Many C.S.A. defenders were also from Ireland.

Losses

Union:	12,700 killed/wounded
C.S.A.:	5,300 killed/wounded

High Tide for the Confederacy

By January 1863, C.S.A. forces had repulsed Union campaigns east and west. In Virginia, it seemed no general could match Robert E. Lee, who stopped Union attempts to take Richmond.

In January, Burnside was replaced by General Joseph Hooker. Confident of success, Hooker moved against Lee. At Chancellorsville, Lee and Jackson whipped him decisively, though they could not destroy his army.

C.S.A. leaders decided an invasion of the North might force the Union to abandon the war. In the West that April, Grant was succeeding in his siege of Vicksburg. The fall of this Mississippi River stronghold would cut off the C.S.A. supply of food and weapons from the Southwest. If Lee successfully invaded the North, it might loosen Grant's chokehold on Vicksburg.

REPULSING PICKETT'S CHARGE
Led by General Lewis Armistead, Confederates in Pickett's Charge break through the Union line on the third day of battle at Gettysburg. Union reinforcements, at left, come up to hammer them back. All along the line the 12,000 attackers were slaughtered or driven back.

January	March	April	May
Emancipation Proclamation takes effect, January 1	Enrollment Act creates an unpopular draft	Grant begins decisive final phase of Vicksburg Campaign	Battle of Chancellorsville
Battle of Stones River			Stonewall Jackson dies
Hooker replaces Burnside			Grant closes the ring around Vicksburg

As Lee's veterans marched through Maryland and into Pennsylvania, alarm filled the Northern states. Lincoln replaced Hooker with General George Meade, a competent veteran. On July 1, Meade caught up to Lee at Gettysburg, and the two armies collided. The war's greatest battle began. Lee ordered frontal attacks that shattered and failed against strong Union positions. After three days of battle, his beaten army was forced to retreat. Meade followed cautiously. He had won a great victory, but Lee was allowed to escape.

On July 4, Grant captured Vicksburg, and the South soon lost control of the Mississippi.

Confederate hopes were revived in September with a great victory at Chickamauga, Georgia. The Union army there was driven back to Chattanooga, Tennessee, and besieged. Then, Grant arrived and defeated the Southern forces. The Union had a true champion in "Sam" Grant, who was soon to become its next commander-in-chief.

PRISONERS OF WAR AT CHATTANOOGA
C.S.A. prisoners are shown at a railroad depot in Chattanooga, Tennessee. C.S.A. forces trapped a Union army in Chattanooga until Grant arrived and broke the siege.

RIOTS IN NEW YORK

In March 1863, Congress passed the Enrollment (Draft) Act, which forced working class white men into the army. Most did not want to fight. The Democratic governor of New York and local leaders fed the anger of poor New Yorkers by giving inflammatory speeches against the draft and the war. On July 13, anti-draft riots raged through the city. Mobs caused widespread destruction and ruled New York for four days. Union troops, some of whom had just fought at Gettysburg, marched in to restore order.

RIOTERS BATTLE THE ARMY
Policemen fought the rioters throughout New York, but could not stop them. Union soldiers came in and fired on the mobs, killing many. As seen in this clash, the rioters did not give up easily.

June	July	September	November
Battle of Brandy Station	Battle of Gettysburg	Battle of Chickamauga	Grant breaks siege of
Lee begins invasion of the	Vicksburg, Port Hudson fall		Chattanooga
North	New York draft riots		Siege of Knoxville,
Meade replaces Hooker	Siege of Charleston fails		Tennessee

Stones River (Murfreesboro), December–January 1862–1863

HARD FIGHT IN TENNESSEE

A Confederate army commanded by General Braxton Bragg invaded Kentucky in August 1862. Panic filled Northern cities as Confederate cavalry raided close to the Ohio state line. Then, in October, General Don Carlos Buell fought the Confederates to a draw at the Battle of Perryville, Kentucky. As Bragg withdrew to Tennessee, Buell was slow to follow. Lincoln soon replaced him with General William Rosecrans.

Under Rosecrans, the Union army marched south toward the strategic railroad junction of Chattanooga, Tennessee. Bragg's army, camped at Murfreesboro, blocked the way. As the Union army drew up, both commanders prepared to attack the other's right wing. In the cold dawn of December 31, the Confederates struck first, routing Union troops who were surprised at breakfast. Rosecrans saw the danger and called off his own planned attack against Bragg's right. Instead he sent reinforcements to the crumbling right wing of his army. Fighting desperately, Union defenders under General Philip Sheridan held on until they ran out of ammunition. The Confederate advance was finally slowed. As darkness fell, charge after charge broke against a newly formed Union line.

Expecting the battered Union army to pull back in the morning, Bragg was surprised to see the enemy still there

HOLDING THE LINE
Union troops on the left of Rosecrans's army break up a Confederate charge. With flags flying, reinforcements march to the rescue of hard-pressed troops on the Union right. Stones River and the railroad to Nashville are in the background.

Losses
Union: 12,906 killed/wounded/missing

C.S.A.: 11,739 killed/wounded/missing

on New Year's Day. Another Confederate assault on January 2 was broken by Union artillery fire. Hearing that Rosecrans had been reinforced, Bragg retreated on the night of January 3, 1863. Union leaders claimed victory, but the Confederates still blocked the path to Chattanooga.

STRUGGLE FOR TENNESSEE
After the Battle of Perryville, Bragg retreated to Tennessee. Rosecrans followed and moved to attack Bragg at Murfreesboro.

▬▬ BRAGG
▬▬ ROSECRANS

BRAGG'S TELESCOPE
Confederate general Braxton Bragg used this field telescope to observe the movements of his troops.

Lens

Canvas covering

THE LEADERSHIP

THE GENERALS OF BOTH ARMIES were experienced. Bragg had fine generals in William Hardee and Leonidas Polk, though he feuded with them. Rosecrans had George Thomas, Alexander McCook, and Thomas Crittenden as corps commanders.

BRAXTON BRAGG (1817-1876)
Bragg was blamed for the failed invasion of Kentucky, and for retreating after Murfreesboro. Later, he was accused of not destroying the Union army after his victory at the Battle of Chickamauga, Georgia. Bragg's subordinate generals did not trust his leadership. Though a good strategist, Bragg had trouble making his officers follow orders.

"The enemy ... is falling back. God has granted us a happy New Year."

—Bragg mistakenly thinking Rosecrans was in retreat

WILLIAM S. ROSECRANS (1819-1898)
Admired for his courage on the battlefield, "Old Rosy" was a popular leader. At Murfreesboro, Rosecrans was everywhere at once. He was faulted for being too slow to follow Bragg after the victory. Rosecrans later outmaneuvered Bragg to capture Chattanooga, but his reputation was ruined after a crushing loss at Chickamauga.

"Bragg's a good dog, but Hold Fast's a better."

—Rosecrans to his troops, referring to himself as "Hold Fast"

KEY TO THE MISSISSIPPI

The Confederate stronghold of Vicksburg, Mississippi, stood on high bluffs overlooking the Mississippi River. Powerful cannon studded the fortifications, prepared to fire down on Union ships that tried to pass. Vicksburg and the fortress of Port Hudson, Louisiana, protected the flow of C.S.A. supplies from the southwest.

From December 1862 through April 1863, Grant struggled to take Vicksburg. Impassable swamps and a strong force under General John C. Pemberton guarded against attack from the north. Finally, in April, Grant risked everything in a daring move to bring his army into position southeast of the city.

While Sherman assaulted Vicksburg's northern defenses, Grant secretly marched the main army down the west bank of the Mississippi. At the same time, Union admiral David Porter ran his fleet of gunboats past deadly fire from Vicksburg's cannon. Porter lost two gunboats getting south of the city. There, he ferried Grant's army across the river.

THE LEADERSHIP

ADMIRAL PORTER'S FLEET PUT GRANT'S ARMY in position to capture Vicksburg. Grant had top generals in Sherman and James McPherson. Pemberton's superiors gave confusing orders: President Davis said hold Vicksburg, while General Joseph Johnston advised abandoning the city.

JOHN C. PEMBERTON (1814–1881)

Northern-born Pemberton defended Vicksburg until his starved and exhausted men threatened rebellion if he did not surrender. Ordered by President Davis to hold out, Pemberton had expected Johnston to come to his relief.

"I know we can get better terms from them on the 4th of July than any other day of the year."

—Pemberton, on negotiating Vicksburg's surrender

DAVID D. PORTER (1813–1891)

A lifelong naval officer, Porter was the son of a commodore. Union admiral David Farragut was his foster brother. Porter took part in several river and coastal operations during the war. He later became superintendent of the Naval Academy.

"Ships cannot crawl up hills 300 feet high, and it is that part of Vicksburg which must be taken by the Army."

—Porter discusses the campaign

Now Grant had a clear path of attack. First, he captured Jackson, Mississippi, cutting off Vicksburg's railroad link to the east. Pemberton sent out an army to stop Grant, but it was driven back. On May 19 and 22, Grant launched unsuccessful frontal assaults against the Vicksburg defenses. The only way to take the city was to starve the defenders out.

For the next two months, Grant's army surrounded Vicksburg, choking off all supplies. On July 4, 1863, with his men weak from hunger, General Pemberton surrendered. Port Hudson fell soon after, and the Mississippi was in Union hands.

▬▬ GRANT'S ATTACK

A RISKY MOVE
After months of trying, Grant could not break through Vicksburg's northern defenses. He marched his men down the west bank of the Mississippi and made a difficult crossing south of Vicksburg.

Light wooden stem

UNION HAND GRENADE
During the long siege, some Union troops threw dartlike hand grenades into enemy defenses. Confederates used artillery shells with lighted fuses as grenades.

Detonation plunger plate exploded the grenade

A COSTLY ATTACK
Union troops charge Confederate defenses at Vicksburg. The assault was hurled back. Grant admitted he blundered by ordering suicidal attacks against the strong Vicksburg defenses. After he surrounded the city, he said, "We will have to dig our way in."

Losses	
Union:	10,142 killed/wounded/missing
C.S.A.:	9,091 killed/wounded/missing

LEE'S GREAT VICTORY

At the end of April, Joseph Hooker led half his 136,000-man Army of the Potomac westward to cross the Rappahannock. John Sedgwick was to cross at Fredericksburg and attack Lee. Thus held in place, Lee would be attacked by Hooker from the west.

Lee did not cooperate, however. He left Jubal Early with 10,000 men at Fredericksburg and led 50,000 troops against Hooker. Surprised by Lee's unexpected advance, Hooker had his army dig in near Chancellorsville, a forested region ten miles from Fredericksburg. He hoped Lee would attack and suffer heavy casualties. Thus, Hooker lost the initiative, and Lee took it. Jackson and Lee made a daring plan to surprise Hooker.

On May 2, Jackson took 26,000 men on a 16-mile march around the Union right. Then he struck and drove the Federals back, inflicting heavy casualties. That evening, while riding through darkness, Jackson was accidentally shot and fatally wounded by his own troops.

Stuart took Jackson's command

A SOLDIER'S PIPE
This briarwood pipe was carved for a Connecticut captain while in camp in April 1863. The officer was killed in action at Chancellorsville three weeks later.

ON THE EVE OF ATTACK
Lee and Jackson meet in deep woods near Chancellorsville on May 1, 1863. Before midnight, J.E.B Stuart rode in to say the Union right was unprotected. Bold plans were made for Jackson to march fast the next day and attack that flank.

Losses	
Union:	17,278 killed/wounded/missing
C.S.A.:	12,821 killed/wounded/missing

and renewed the assaults. Hooker was knocked out of action by a shell exploding nearby, and his army fought defensively. Sedgwick broke through at Fredericksburg, fighting his way toward Hooker. Lee turned to face Sedgwick and, along with Early, drove him back across the river. Hooker lost heart and also retreated.

Federal forces again withdrew from the Rappahannock, and Hooker was replaced by George Meade. Chancellorsville is considered Lee's most brilliant victory, but it was costly. A quarter of his force were casualties. Further, he lost the irreplaceable Stonewall Jackson.

HOOKER BEATEN AT CHANCELLORSVILLE
To avoid Lee's defenses at Fredericksburg, Hooker maneuvered part of his army westward across the Rappahannock. Lee countered and met Hooker at Chancellorsville.

THE LEADERSHIP

GENERAL ROBERT RODES'S DIVISION led the way in Jackson's devastating attack. General Oliver Howard's corps took the brunt of the attack. Hooker faulted Howard for not being prepared, but this general redeemed himself in Atlanta and the West.

"I made frequent demonstrations to induce the enemy to attack me, but he would not accept my challenge."

—Hooker, saying he withdrew because he was out of rations, and Lee would not attack

JOSEPH HOOKER (1814-1879)
General Hooker was a West Pointer who fought in the Seminole and Mexican wars. He was a corps commander before leading the Army of the Potomac. After Chancellorsville, he served with distinction in the western theater and the Atlanta Campaign.

"Order A.P. Hill to prepare for action—pass the infantry to the front rapidly . . ."

—The delirious Jackson's dying words

THOMAS J. JACKSON (1824-1863)
Lee's army was organized in two corps: Jackson led one, Longstreet the other. After playing key roles at Second Bull Run, Antietam, and Fredericksburg, Jackson reached the peak of success with his Chancellorsville attack. In that battle, he was accidentally shot by his own men.

BLUE COATS WIN RESPECT

After Chancellorsville, Lee hoped to end the war with one great victory. He began marching his army out of Fredericksburg, preparing to invade the North. Suspecting that Lee was planning a major move, Hooker ordered his cavalry to search for the main C.S.A. army.

Southern troopers, or cavalrymen, under famed commander Jeb Stuart, were considered superior to the Union cavalry. After two years of war, the Union cavalry had become stronger and was ready to challenge Stuart. When General Hooker sent them out

to find Lee, they were eager to go.

At first light on June 6, a force of 11,000 men, mostly cavalry, splashed across fords on the Rappahannock River. Commanding general Alfred Pleasonton moved toward Brandy Station in two columns. The Union attack surprised C.S.A. cavalry patrolling along the river. They were at first driven back in confusion. Stuart and his officers rallied their men, and the battle began.

For 12 hours, sabers flashed and hoofbeats thundered in charge and counter-charge. The Union cavalry

THE LEADERSHIP

PLEASONTON'S COMMANDERS INCLUDED JOHN BUFORD and John Gregg. Stuart's were W.E. Jones, Fitzhugh Lee, Wade Hampton, and R.E. Lee's son, General William H.F. "Rooney" Lee, who was badly wounded. Lee recovered to rejoin the army.

JAMES E.B. "JEB" STUART (1833–1864)

Stuart was Lee's dashing commander of cavalry. Daring rides around McClellan's army won him fame and embarrassed Northern leaders. Lee depended on Stuart for information about enemy movements. Stuart was killed in action just after the 1864 Battle of Spotsylvania.

"Tell General Jones to attend to the Yankees in his front, and I'll watch the flanks."

—Stuart, dismissing Jones's report that enemy cavalry are about to attack

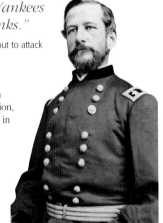

ALFRED PLEASONTON (1824–1897)

A U.S. cavalry officer before the Civil War, Pleasonton commanded at Antietam, Fredericksburg, Brandy Station, Chancellorsville, and Gettysburg. He finished the war in Missouri, where he fought against Sterling Price.

"[O]ver and through them we rode, sabering as we went."

—U.S. cavalry officer, describing the fight at Brandy Station

showed skill and courage in the long struggle as Stuart's men fought furiously to hold the field. In the end, Pleasonton retreated. Stuart had won, but he had been caught unprepared and almost defeated. The Union cavalry had proven it could take him on.

Though they had lost the greatest cavalry battle of the war, the Union troopers had completed their task by finding Lee's army. Hooker now realized Lee was planning an invasion.

SURPRISE ATTACK
Union cavalry dashed across the Rappahannock, catching C.S.A. troopers by surprise and pushing them back to Brandy Station, Virginia. Lee's main army was camped just to the west at Culpeper, Virginia.

■■■ STUART ■■■ PLEASONTON

C.S.A. CAVALRY SABER
Like most edged weapons manufactured in the South during the war, this saber was crudely made. Yet, in the hands of a determined Southern trooper, it was deadly.

GRAY COMANCHES
The 35th Virginia Cavalry, known as "Comanches" because their fierce war cry sounded like a Comanche war whoop, charge a New York battery. Colonel Elijah V. White, mounted on his gray horse, "Lige," leads his men to help turn the tide against the Union forces near Brandy Station.

Losses

Union: 930 killed/wounded/missing

C.S.A.:   485 killed/wounded/missing

LEE INVADES THE NORTH

After the victory at Chancellorsville, President Davis and General Lee agreed to invade the North. Lee seemed invincible. Also, people in the Northern states were questioning the cost of the war. One great victory on Northern soil might convince the Union to give up the struggle.

Lee moved north in early June, and Hooker followed. Jeb Stuart's cavalry began a long raid around Hooker's army. Stuart hoped to recover his reputation after being outfought at Brandy Station. Lee hoped he would soon return. Without Stuart's cavalry to scout, Lee could not know where the main Union force was. Lee continued into Pennsylvania before Stuart returned.

On June 28, Hooker was replaced by General George Meade. After the Chancellorsville defeat, Lincoln wanted Hooker removed. Meade quickly placed his army to block Lee's path to the south. A major battle seemed inevitable. It came on July 1, when A.P. Hill's men entered the town of Gettysburg and crashed into John Buford's cavalry scouting for the Union army.

Though outnumbered, Buford fought hard. He held his ground until

20TH MAINE BATTLEFIELD PAROLE
A parole allowed a captured soldier to go free as long as he promised not to fight again. This parole was given to a member of the 20th Maine who was captured during the fighting at Gettysburg.

"DON'T GIVE AN INCH!"
On the second day of fighting, Union troops came up just in time to stop an enemy move to take undefended Little Round Top. This strategic hill overlooked Union lines. Waving a riding crop, Union officer Strong Vincent yelled, "Don't give an inch!" as his men defended the rocky crest.

Losses

Union:	9,000 killed/wounded/ missing
C.S.A.:	6,500 killed/wounded/missing

reinforced by infantry under General John Reynolds. The C.S.A. drove the Union troops back and killed Reynolds. Meade's main army still had not come up, and his advance force at Gettysburg was outnumbered. Late in the day, Lee proposed that General Richard Ewell attack the Federals. If possible, Ewell could capture the high ground on Cemetery Hill. Ewell decided the move was too risky and held his men back. Lee planned a massive attack for the next day.

INVASION!
Lee launched an invasion of the North from Fredericksburg, Virginia, and marched through Maryland into Pennsylvania. Hooker followed close behind. He was soon replaced by Meade. At Gettysburg, Pennsylvania, the armies clashed in the most famous battle of the war.

▬▬▬ LEE   ▬▬▬ MEADE

THE LEADERSHIP

GENERAL JOHN BUFORD LED THE FEDERAL cavalrymen who held off the first C.S.A. advance. He fought General Henry Heth, who led A.P. Hill's division while Hill led a corps. James Archer became the first C.S.A. general captured since Lee took command.

RICHARD S. EWELL (1817–1872)
A West Pointer, Ewell was a key part of Stonewall Jackson's greatest victories. When Jackson was killed, Ewell was promoted, but was not as successful in higher command. He was blamed for not attacking aggressively on the first day of Gettysburg. Captured after the fall of Richmond in 1865, Ewell survived the war.

"They will attack you in the morning and they will come booming...."
—Buford to an officer at Gettysburg

JOHN F. REYNOLDS (1820–1863)
Reynolds was considered by many to be one of the Union's finest officers. He was a West Point graduate. Reynolds was a candidate to replace Hooker as head of the Army of the Potomac. Before accepting command, Reynolds demanded more freedom from President Lincoln's control. Lincoln could not promise this, and chose George Meade instead.

"General Meade will make no blunder on my front."
—Lee, on George Meade as new commander of the Union Army

PICKETT'S CHARGE

Meade brought up the main Union army late on July 1, reinforcing the troops that had fought that day. He was determined not to retreat.

On July 2, Lee ordered a massive assault all along the Union line. His right wing managed to penetrate the line in places, but Union troops plugged these gaps. The Federals were skillfully led by generals such as Winfield S. Hancock and John Gibbon. The Confederates almost took Little Round Top, the undefended high ground overlooking the Union line. Union officers saw the danger just in time and rushed

troops to hold the hill. The C.S.A. attacks captured ground but were stopped after heavy losses.

Lee's generals argued that more frontal attacks were hopeless, but Lee was sure he could break through. He ordered another assault for July 3.

Longstreet, with George Pickett's fresh troops, attacked the center of the Union line this time. C.S.A. infantry,

BATTLE DRUM

This Union drum was found on the battlefield. Drummer boys beat out commands to direct the movements of the troops. Drummers were usually young boys, some only nine or 10 years old.

Hand-painted eagle and crest

Losses:	for all three days
Union:	3,155 killed 14,529 wounded 5,365 missing
C.S.A.:	3,903 killed 18,735 wounded 5,425 missing

NORTH CAROLINA'S ASSAULT

C.S.A. troops under General Isaac Trimble charge on the third day of Gettysburg. These North Carolina men attacked alongside Pickett's troops. Rail fences lining a road slowed the Carolinians, and most were shot down before they reached enemy lines. Some got to the Union positions but were driven back in defeat.

12,000 strong, charged across a half-mile of open field. Union artillery ripped holes in their lines, but they continued to come on until mowed down by rifle fire. In one place, the attackers broke the Union line, but reinforcements came up and drove them back. "Pickett's Charge," Lee's great assault, had failed.

In the following days, the crippled Confederate Army escaped across the Potomac into Virginia. Meade followed cautiously. Though Lee's army was not destroyed, the North had won a great victory. The end of the war seemed farther away than ever for the Confederacy as their defeated army marched home.

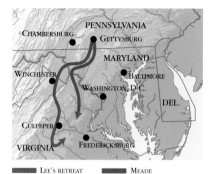

▬▬▬ LEE'S RETREAT   ▬▬▬ MEADE

ESCAPING DESTRUCTION
After the three-day Battle of Gettysburg, Lee's battered army retreated southward. Meade followed, but his army was also badly hurt. Lincoln felt Meade missed the chance to destroy Lee's weakened army and end the war.

THE LEADERSHIP

LONGSTREET DISAGREED WITH LEE and did not want to frontally assault the strong enemy positions. Union officer Joshua Chamberlain was awarded the Medal of Honor for holding back determined C.S.A. attacks on the second day.

"[N]o 15,000 men ever arrayed for battle can take that position."

—Longstreet to Lee, protesting the order to attack on the third day

GEORGE E. PICKETT (1825–1875)
Pickett graduated last in his class at West Point, but won honors for bravery in the Mexican War. He became Longstreet's favorite officer. On the third day at Gettysburg, Pickett led Longstreet's troops in the great charge. Though not all the men were under Pickett's direct command, he won fame for the assault, which became known as "Pickett's Charge." He survived the charge and the war.

"If Lee attacks tomorrow, it will be on your front."

—Meade to General John Gibbon the night before Pickett's Charge

GEORGE C. MEADE (1815–1872)
A West Pointer and Mexican War veteran, Meade performed well commanding troops under McClellan and Hooker. Lincoln was disappointed that Meade failed to destroy Lee's army after Gettysburg. When Grant became general-in-chief, Meade remained in command of the Army of the Potomac. Grant, as the superior officer, made all key decisions. In his memoirs, Grant complimented Meade for dealing well with this difficult relationship.

THE LAST RIVER FORTRESS

With possession of New Orleans, the Union wanted to take the two remaining Southern strong points on the Mississippi: Port Hudson and

> *"That's another damn Yankee lie!"*
>
> —Rebel defender of Port Hudson, when told Vicksburg had fallen

RIVER CAMPAIGN
In the spring, Federal forces converged on Port Hudson, 25 miles north of Baton Rouge. Port Hudson and Vicksburg blocked Union travel on the Mississippi.

■■■ BANKS

Vicksburg. Grant moved on Vicksburg in early 1863, and by late May General Nathaniel Banks was attacking Port Hudson. The 7,200 Port Hudson defenders suffered hunger and illness. Still, they held on, repelling bloody frontal attacks launched by Banks. Two such attacks cost 4,000 Union dead and wounded. Many more Union men fell ill with fever or sunstroke. Vicksburg gave up on July 4, and Port Hudson's commander, General Franklin Gardner, surrendered on July 9.

THE LEADERSHIP

THE INCOMPETENT BANKS lost battles from the Shenandoah to the Red River in Texas. He benefited at Port Hudson from the naval gunners of David Farragut's fleet.

FRANKLIN GARDNER (1823-1873)
A native New Yorker and a West Pointer, Gardner moved South and became a C.S.A. commander. He led both infantry and cavalry. After Port Hudson, Gardner was exchanged and returned to duty.

Losses

Union:	3,000 killed/wounded/missing
C.S.A.:	1,700 killed/wounded/missing, 5,500 prisoners

SHRAPNEL-DENTED UNION
DRINKING CUP

A STORM OF GUNFIRE
Port Hudson's artillery batteries blast away at Flag Officer David Farragut's fleet in March. Farragut broke through, but lost the USS *Mississippi*.

NAVY REPULSED IN CAROLINA

Gaining control of the fine harbor of Charleston, South Carolina, was an important Union goal. Charleston had begun the war by firing on Fort Sumter, and the Union also wanted to take revenge on the city.

Charleston's defenses depended on stout coastal forts and artillery batteries. From mid-June 1862, the

> *"[The] bells and whistles [told] that the shell had fallen in the city."*
>
> —Union officer, about the long-range shelling of Charleston

Union navy and army laid siege to the city. Admiral John Dahlgren's ironclads bombarded her forts to rubble, but the Confederates would not surrender. On July 18, 1863, an assault on Fort Wagner was bloodily defeated.

Charleston held out even after the forts were lost and the city itself came under bombardment. She surrendered in February 1865, as Sherman's army approached.

SOLID DEFENSES
Charleston's coastal forts prevented the Union navy from entering the harbor. The city was under siege from 1862 until early 1865.

THE LEADERSHIP

UNION GENERAL QUINCY GILLMORE led troops at Charleston in 1863. He manufactured 400 medals for gallantry and gave them to enlisted men. General Pierre Beauregard skillfully defended Charleston.

GILLMORE MEDAL

JOHN A. DAHLGREN (1809–1870)
A career naval officer, Admiral Dahlgren commanded a Union Atlantic squadron. He invented the powerful Dahlgren Gun, used by the navy. Dahlgren led naval forces in the Charleston siege.

DEATH ON THE PARAPET
The 54th Massachusetts commander, Colonel Robert Shaw, is killed in the doomed July 18 assault on Fort Wagner. The 54th was one of the first African-American regiments created during the war.

Losses	
Union:	1,993 killed/wounded/missing
C.S.A.:	218 killed/wounded/missing

SOUTHERN VICTORY IN WEST

Things were going badly for the South by August 1863. In the western theater, the Mississippi Valley was under Union control. Yet nearby C.S.A. forces were still fighting hard. At Chattanooga, Tennessee, General Braxton Bragg prepared to take on the Union Army of the Cumberland, led by William Rosecrans.

In early September, Rosecrans crossed the Tennessee River with 58,000 men and advanced into northern Georgia. He planned to bring Bragg to battle. Bragg was strengthened to more than 66,000. In his reinforcements was Longstreet's corps, which arrived by train from the eastern theater. The armies met near Chickamauga Creek on September 19 in a great battle.

The struggle raged along a six-mile front, and night ended the fighting. The next day, Bragg attacked. A weakness accidentally developed in the Union line as troops were being maneuvered. By coincidence, Longstreet attacked at this very moment and broke through. He shattered the Federal right wing.

Thinking the battle was lost, Rosecrans and most of his army began fleeing to Chattanooga.

ILLINOIS REGIMENTAL BUGLE
This German-made silver bugle was presented by five friends to a private in the 21st Illinois. One friend was killed soon after, when the regiment was decimated at Chickamauga.

CLOSE-QUARTER FIGHTING
Union troops take heavy losses in exchanges of volleys at the Battle of Chickamauga in northern Georgia. Braxton Bragg drove the Federals from the field and followed them to Chattanooga, Tennessee, for another round.

Losses

Union:	1,657 killed, 9,756 wounded, 4,757 missing
C.S.A.:	2,312 dead, 14,674 wounded, 1,468 missing

Bragg would have routed the Federals and caused much more loss except that General George Thomas did not retreat. Thomas and several other commanders stubbornly held their ground until nightfall. This prevented the destruction of the Union army. After dark, Thomas withdrew and rejoined Rosecrans. Bragg immediately advanced and laid siege to Chattanooga.

After Chickamauga, Rosecrans and other generals who had retreated were removed from command. Thomas, now nicknamed the "Rock of Chickamauga," replaced Rosecrans.

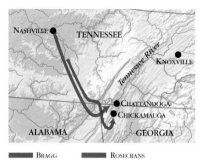

BRAGG   ROSECRANS

LONG MARCHES TO BATTLE
Bragg moved to Chattanooga and was reinforced while Rosecrans maneuvered to cut his supply lines. Their engagement at Chickamauga ended with a C.S.A. victory.

THE LEADERSHIP

Bragg had the services of Lee's "warhorse," General James Longstreet. Yet, Bragg's unstable personality led him to relieve several fine officers from command. These included D.H. Hill and Leonidas Polk, who had criticized him.

GEORGE H. THOMAS (1816–1870)
A Virginian, General Thomas graduated West Point and later was an instructor there. He was a veteran of the Seminole and Mexican wars and served in the cavalry with several future C.S.A. generals, including Robert E. Lee.

"I am going to Thomas, orders or no orders!"

—General Gordon Granger, who rushed to join Thomas's stand

DANIEL H. HILL (1821–1889)
West Pointer Hill was a Mexican War veteran and a mathematics professor. General Hill served the C.S.A. with distinction before joining Bragg. Hill reported Bragg as incompetent, and Bragg took away his troops. Hill went on to serve under Joseph Johnston.

"Disapproved. Shooters are more needed than tooters."

—Hill answers a soldier's request for transfer to the band

GRANT BREAKS THE SIEGE

Bragg cut the supply lines of Thomas's Army of the Cumberland, trapped in Chattanooga. The Federals began to starve. Ulysses S. Grant took command of Union operations in the region and hurried by back roads into Chattanooga.

Reinforcements were sent from William T. Sherman's forces and from the Army of the Potomac. Sherman's veterans had taken Vicksburg, and the eastern troops had won at Gettysburg. None of these troops had high regard for the Army of the Cumberland. Thomas's men had something to prove.

Grant's first move was to open Chattanooga's supply lines. Late in October, he sent a force on rafts down the Tennessee River to capture a key ferry crossing. This reestablished supply to the city. In mid-November, Joseph Hooker captured important C.S.A. positions on lofty Lookout Mountain. Bragg still remained strongly fortified on Missionary Ridge, overlooking the city.

HARDTACK
Hardtack crackers were called "worm castles" because maggots often infested them. Hardtack was the Union soldier's basic food, crumbled and mixed with soup, fried in grease, or eaten dry.

Losses

Union: 753 killed, 4,722 wounded, 349 missing

C.S.A.: 361 killed, 2,160 wounded, 4,146 missing

AN UNSTOPPABLE CHARGE
Army of the Cumberland attackers push up Missionary Ridge and rout Confederate defenders at Chattanooga in November 1863. This was yet another devastating loss for the failing Confederate cause.

On November 25, Thomas assaulted Bragg's lines at the base of Missionary Ridge. Meanwhile, Sherman led the main attack against the Confederate right. Sherman's attack stalled, but Thomas captured the base of the ridge. Then his men kept going up the hill. Without orders, they braved murderous fire and drove the enemy from Missionary Ridge.

William Hardee's corps skillfully covered the Confederate retreat, but Bragg was beaten. The Army of the Cumberland had proven itself the equal of any other Union force.

BRAGG   GRANT

THE SIEGE OF CHATTANOOGA

Before Grant broke out, C.S.A. forces under Bragg had the Union army trapped against the Tennessee River in Chattanooga, Tennessee.

THE LEADERSHIP

JOSEPH HOOKER, DEFEATED AT CHANCELLORSVILLE, played a major role at Chattanooga. His troops stormed Lookout Mountain, setting the stage for further attacks. Patrick Cleburne stopped Sherman's main attack, but that was not enough for a Confederate victory.

WILLIAM J. HARDEE (1815-1873)

West Pointer Hardee attended a French cavalry academy. A Seminole and Mexican wars veteran, he was an instructor at West Point. He served in the C.S.A.'s western theater campaigns and later against Sherman. Hardee joined Joseph Johnston, and fought to the end of the war.

"[Bragg was] cursing like a sailor."

—An observer, as Union troops kept on charging up Missionary Ridge

PHILIP H. SHERIDAN (1831-1888)

A leader in the Missionary Ridge assault, General Sheridan almost captured Bragg himself. A West Pointer, Sheridan entered the war as a lieutenant, and eventually became one of the best Union generals. As a daring cavalry commander, he was crucial to Grant's success.

"Chickamauga! Chickamauga!"

—The battle cry of Thomas's Army of the Potomac

Total War in the Confederacy

The tide of war had turned against the Confederacy by the start of 1864. On every front the Union was growing stronger, but for the men and their leaders many fierce battles still lay ahead.

The Mississippi was under Union control. Southern seaports were being captured or blockaded. C.S.A. forces had been driven from Tennessee. After Gettysburg, Lee no longer seemed invincible. Taking overall command of the Union army was Ulysses S. Grant, who had won many great victories in the West.

Lincoln and Grant planned a broad push on every front. This fall, Lincoln would be up for reelection. His opponent was Democrat George B. McClellan, former commander of the Army of the Potomac. McClellan wanted to end the fighting and negotiate peace. Without battlefield victories, Lincoln might lose the presidency.

BATTLE OF ATLANTA
James McPherson's Army of the Tennessee clashes with John Hood's forces east of Atlanta in July. Hood was driven back with a loss of 10,000 men. The Union lost only 3,800, but McPherson was killed in the fighting.

March	May	June	July
Lincoln appoints Grant commander-in-chief of all Union armies	Battle of the Wilderness	Battle of Cold Harbor	Hood replaces Johnston
Red River Campaign begins	Battle of Spotsylvania	USS *Kearsarge* fights CSS *Alabama*	Battle of Atlanta
	Sherman begins advance on Atlanta	Battle of Kennesaw Mountain	Battle of the Crater during Siege of Petersburg

Grant began to march around Lee, to make him to do the attacking. Lee cleverly countered Grant's moves, and usually it was Union men who were slaughtered in frontal attacks. Names that once belonged to sleepy villages and dusty crossroads now meant battlefields and bloodshed. The Wilderness. Spotsylvania Courthouse. Cold Harbor. Petersburg. To the soldiers, the horrors of war were all too common as they fought on, month after month.

The year wore down, and Lincoln got the victories he needed to be reelected: Atlanta, Mobile Bay, and the Shenandoah Valley. Now, it was only a matter of time before Grant would do what McClellan had not: capture Richmond.

RUNNING THE BLOCKADE

Britain's textile industry needed Southern cotton, and the South needed British armaments. Fast Confederate merchant ships risked the Northern blockade and dashed out of port with cotton. Then they would slip back in with guns and ammunition. Success brought a ship's owner a fortune. Failure meant being sunk or captured. The Southern blockade runners made 8,000 successful trips.

SPEED AGAINST POWER
The blockade runner *Sumter* flees from the patrolling Union warship *Brooklyn;* in August, the *Brooklyn* took part in Farragut's victory at Mobile Bay.

IN THE TRENCHES
A rifle pit shelters weatherbeaten Union soldiers campaigning in northern Virginia. Officers study the surroundings while, in the background, gunners are busy with field artillery. This photograph was taken at Fredericksburg, Virginia.

August	September	November	December
Battle of Mobile Bay, Alabama	Atlanta falls to Sherman	Lincoln is reelected	Battle of Nashville, Tennessee
	Sheridan's Shenandoah Valley Campaign begins	Sherman's March to the Sea begins at Atlanta	Sherman occupies Savannah, Georgia
		Battle of Franklin, Tennessee	

DEFEAT ON THE RED

C.S.A. troops under General E. Kirby Smith protected East Texas. From ports there, Confederates traded cotton for foreign-made rifles.

Lincoln ordered an invasion of Texas. He hoped to stop the flow of weapons. Also, French armies had invaded Mexico in a move the United States considered to be threatening. Lincoln wanted U.S. troops in Texas to protect the Mexican border.

In March, the biggest invasion force ever seen in western waters began to move up Louisiana's Red River toward Texas. General Nathaniel Banks commanded 27,000 troops, and Admiral David Porter had a fleet of 20 gunboats.

Smith sent General Richard Taylor, his best commander, to stop Banks. Taylor was outnumbered, but took advantage of Banks's incompetence. In April, Taylor defeated Banks at the Battle of Sabine Cross Roads. The next day, Taylor attacked at Pleasant Hill, hoping to destroy the Union force. C.S.A. troops were close to victory

THE LEADERSHIP

RICHARD TAYLOR HAD SERVED UNDER JACKSON in his 1862 Valley Campaign. Colonel Joseph Bailey won the thanks of Congress for saving the Union fleet. West Pointer William Franklin was a corps commander under Banks.

NATHANIEL P. BANKS (1816–1894)
A former U.S. Congressman and three-term governor of Massachusetts, Banks got his command because of political connections. Though badly beaten by Jackson in the 1862 Valley Campaign, he captured Port Hudson in 1863. Banks lost field command after his failure on the Red River. He was again elected to Congress after the war.

"Don't you know this is mutiny?"

—William Franklin to A.J. Smith, who proposed Franklin arrest Banks for retreating, and take command himself

"...had Banks followed up his success vigorously, he would have met but feeble opposition to his advance on Shreveport."

—Kirby Smith, on the Battle of Pleasant Hill

EDMUND KIRBY SMITH (1824–1893)
Mexican War veteran and West Pointer Kirby Smith invaded Kentucky with Bragg in 1862. He then took command of forces west of the Mississippi. When Vicksburg fell, the West was cut off from government control. Kirby Smith ruled almost independently, and the area became called "Kirby Smithdom." Kirby Smith surrendered the last C.S.A. force in June 1865.

when Union veteran Andrew J. Smith brought up his troops and smashed their assault. Smith was sure he could counterattack and destroy Taylor, but Banks had lost confidence and abandoned the invasion. The Union army and Porter's gunboats began a long retreat.

Taylor pursued boldly with his small force, making slashing attacks on Union columns. Then disaster loomed as the water level of the Red River fell, trapping the Union fleet in shallow water. There seemed no escape until engineering officer Joseph Bailey put 3,000 soldiers to work and dammed the river. The water rose and the fleet steamed on. Bailey saved the Union fleet, but Kirby Smith kept control of Texas.

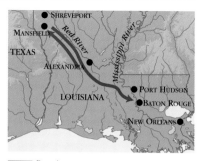

BANKS'S ADVANCE AND RETREAT

BASE FOR INVADING TEXAS

Banks planned to steam up the Red River from Alexandria, Louisiana, and capture Shreveport near the Texas border. This would serve as a base for an invasion of East Texas. Defeated, Banks made a speedy retreat, harassed all the way by aggressive C.S.A. forces.

COMMANDER'S UNIFORM COAT

Banks always looked the part of a commanding general. He was well-dressed in polished boots, handsome gloves, and tailored clothes. He wore this uniform coat at the Siege of Port Hudson, in 1863.

A CAPTURED STEAMER

The *General Stirling Price,* named after a C.S.A. officer, was a wooden steamer converted into a fighting ram. She was sunk in a fight at Memphis, Tennessee, and restored to become a Union warship with the shortened name *General Price*. She served as Admiral Porter's flagship during the Red River Campaign.

Losses

Union:	approximately 4,600 killed/wounded/missing
C.S.A.:	4,900 killed/wounded/missing

THROUGH FIRE AND DEATH

In March, Ulysses S. Grant went east to take command of the Union armies. He and Lincoln planned to defeat the Confederacy by striking at its heart. This meant total war, destroying food and crops, and tearing up railroad tracks that carried men and supplies.

It also meant costly frontal attacks. Unlike the North, the South could not replace casualties. By May, new battles showed Grant's willingness to sacrifice soldiers and wear down Lee's army.

Grant directed the 120,000-man Army of the Potomac—led by George Meade—right at Lee, who had 70,000.

While other actions were pressed in the Shenandoah and on the Peninsula, Grant and Meade forced a fight. On May 4, the armies met in the forested "Wilderness" region of Virginia. A bloody close-quarters struggle raged for two days. Both armies fought on, despite heavy casualties.

On the second day, John Gregg's Texas troops were key to an attack that shattered part of the Union left. Lee rode forward to lead the Texans in this attack, but they yelled it was too dangerous. One Texan took the bridle of Lee's horse and turned the animal

THE LEADERSHIP

JAMES LONGSTREET WAS WOUNDED and remained out of action for six months, a serious loss. General Winfield Hancock, commanding a Union wing, recovered from a powerful attack and repulsed the Confederates. Such determination made the battle end in a draw.

JOHN GREGG (1828-1864)
A member of the C.S.A. congress from Texas, General Gregg was captured at Fort Donelson and later exchanged. Wounded at Chickamauga, Gregg also fought at Spotsylvania, and Petersburg. He was killed in action in October 1864.

"We won't go on unless you go back!"

—Gregg's Texans, stopping R.E. Lee from leading an attack

WINFIELD SCOTT HANCOCK (1824-1886)
A veteran of the Mexican and Seminole wars, Hancock was a West Pointer and a career officer. He fought in the eastern campaigns and was wounded at Gettysburg. Hancock ran unsuccessfully for president in 1880, losing to former general John Garfield.

"Many men from both armies, looking for water during the night, found themselves within the opposite lines."

—Union general Andrew Humphreys, remembering the Wilderness

around, indicating that Lee should go back. (A similar incident occurred later, at Spotsylvania.)

Lee lost Longstreet in the Wilderness battle. Longstreet was accidentally wounded by his own men on May 6, one year after Stonewall Jackson was shot the same way. Grant and Lee attacked and counterattacked, until both exhausted armies broke off the fighting. Grant's losses were almost double Lee's, but the Union had kept the offensive. The struggle immediately moved on to Spotsylvania.

INTO THE FOREST
The advance of Grant and Meade in May 1864 brought Lee to battle west of Fredericksburg in the dense woods known as the Wilderness. The fighting was bloody but inconclusive.

COMMANDER IN THE FORE
Colonel George Ryan leads his 140th New York across a bullet-swept field during the Wilderness fighting. The 140th suffered heavy casualties and had to retreat. Then the woods caught fire, consuming the dead and many wounded.

POCKET WATCH
This silver pocket watch belonged to a Vermonter who was mortally wounded in 1864 at Cold Harbor, Virginia. He later died aboard a ship on the Potomac River, according to the inscription.

Losses	
Union:	2,246 killed, 12,073 wounded
C.S.A.:	7,750 killed/wounded

THE BLOODY ANGLE

The Wilderness fighting ended, and Grant and Lee maneuvered southeastward to take the crossroads at Spotsylvania Court House. The armies hurried through darkness as forest fires raged around them. If Grant reached the crossroads first, he would be between Lee and Richmond. Lee must stop him from moving on the Confederate capital.

Grant aimed to take a defensive position and force Lee to attack, but the Union advance was delayed by Southern cavalry. Lee was ready for Grant's first assaults on May 7. Lee's trenches and fences formed a horseshoe facing Grant's army. On

May 10, Grant charged a strongpoint that bulged out from the rest. Young Colonel Emory Upton led a dozen regiments forward and broke through. Upton was driven back by a counterattack, but Grant was impressed by the officer's ability.

The strongpoint was next to a fortified angle of rail fencing that became the object of both armies. On a rainy May 12, the struggle for this "Bloody Angle" was the fiercest hand-to-hand fighting of the Civil War. C.S.A. general John Gordon's division counterattacked a Union breakthrough here, and the dead piled up. Between clashes, weary men often huddled on opposite sides of the fence, just a few yards apart.

BLOODY ANGLE
Federals attack Confederates defending a position known as the "Bloody Angle," near Spotsylvania Court House. Fighting here surged back and forth, as Grant relentlessly tried to destroy Lee's army.

Losses	
Union:	10,920 killed/wounded/missing
C.S.A.:	Unknown

The campaign wore on without a decisive victory, but Grant lost John Sedgwick, a top commander. Sedgwick was shot while standing in an exposed position where enemy snipers were picking off soldiers. By May 20, Grant's army was again slipping to the south, looking for an opening around Lee's left. Lee kept blocking his way. In this time, Philip Sheridan's Union cavalry rode on a raid toward Richmond. On May 24, Sheridan clashed at Yellow Tavern with Jeb Stuart, who was mortally wounded. One more of Lee's best lieutenants was gone.

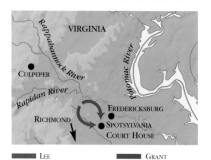

LEE   GRANT

MOVE AND FIGHT AGAIN
Grant did not let up after the Wilderness, but immediately renewed the battle with Lee at Spotsylvania Court House on May 7. This ferocious campaign lasted two long weeks, ending in a draw.

THE LEADERSHIP

NEW YORK COLONEL EMORY UPTON so impressed Grant that he was promoted to general. A West Pointer, Upton was just 24 years of age. Lee's troops were led by Richard Ewell, Jubal Early, and Richard Anderson. Including Jeb Stuart, Lee lost nine generals, who were either killed, wounded, or captured.

"Men would sometimes go out under a severe fire, in the hope of finding a full haversack."
—C.S.A. general, describing hungry troops taking supplies from Union dead

JOHN B. GORDON (1832-1904)
General Gordon was a Georgia lawyer who became colonel of an Alabama regiment. He rose to brigadier general after Antietam. His campaigns included the Peninsula, Chancellorsville, Gettysburg, the Wilderness, Petersburg, and Appomattox.

JOHN SEDGWICK (1813-1864)
One the best-loved Union corps commanders, General John Sedgwick was killed at Spotsylvania. Sedgwick was a West Pointer and a career officer, who served in Indian wars and the Mexican War. In the Civil War's eastern campaigns, he was wounded twice.

"They couldn't hit an elephant at this distance."
—Sedgwick, moments before being killed by a sharpshooter

A DOOMED ASSAULT

Grant wanted an all-out battle in which overwhelming Union numbers would triumph. Lee intended to fight defensively and inflict heavy

> *"I have always regretted that the last assault at Cold Harbor was ever made."*

—Grant, in his memoirs about Cold Harbor

LEE PROTECTS RICHMOND
Grant tried to get past Lee as they maneuvered to Cold Harbor. Each time, Lee arrived first and prepared a strong position.

LEE
GRANT

Union casualties. Lee would not yield important ground without a fight. At Cold Harbor, Grant brought that fight to him in brutal frontal attacks. On June 3rd, 7,000 Union men fell in half an hour. General Francis Barlow's division broke into Lee's defenses, but was driven back. Still, Grant sent wave after wave of soldiers into battle. In the end, Cold Harbor was a stalemate. Grant had 108,000 men against Lee's 59,000, but did not make the most of his advantage. Instead, he ordered doomed frontal attacks that lasted only a few minutes, yet cost thousands of casualties.

THE LEADERSHIP

A.P. HILL AND RICHARD ANDERSON bore the brunt of the Union attacks. Anderson, leading the wounded Longstreet's corps, repulsed 14 assaults before 8 AM They faced the 50,000 men of three Union corps, including General William Smith's, which had 3,000 casualties.

FRANCIS C. BARLOW (1834–1896)
First in his class at Harvard, General Barlow enlisted as a private in a New York regiment. He soon was commissioned lieutenant colonel and promoted to general. Barlow was severely wounded at Antietam and Gettysburg.

UNHESITATING HEROISM
Maine artillerymen fighting as infantry rush Lee's lines; Grant tried to overwhelm Lee by sheer numbers, but Lee threw back Grant's attacks causing heavy Union losses.

Losses

Union: (May–June) 50,000 casualties

C.S.A.: (May–June) 32,000 casualties

WAR IN THE TRENCHES

In mid-June, Grant moved southward and made for Petersburg. This railroad junction was key to Lee's supply lines. P.G.T. Beauregard and just 2,200 men blocked the first Union attack on Petersburg. Grant's subordinates delayed in making a full assault, giving Lee time to send reinforcements. Both armies then dug in with strong fortifications. On July 30, a mine full of explosives blew up under a Confederate position. The accompanying Union assault failed, as William Mahone's troops counterattacked. The Petersburg campaign, with many actions, lasted through May 1865. It was a war of trenches and artillery bombardments. Firing went on hour after hour, and both armies lived in unending mud and filth.

"Hell itself…
simply awful."

—A Union officer, on enduring the siege

VIRGINIA

COLD HARBOR

RICHMOND

James River

PETERSBURG

ADVANCE ON PETERSBURG
Grant kept forcing Lee to shift his defenses. Faking a drive south, Grant swung his main force east, then back toward Petersburg, 20 miles below Richmond. Lee rushed to stop him.

▬ LEE

▬ GRANT

THE LEADERSHIP

BEAUREGARD ONCE AGAIN APPEARED at a crucial moment as he fought off the first Union attack on Petersburg. Meade continued as Grant's field commander of the Army of the Potomac.

WILLIAM MAHONE (1826–1895)
A Virginia Military Institute graduate, Mahone was promoted for his defense at the "Battle of the Crater." He proved to be Lee's most outstanding division commander throughout the rest of the war.

DIGGING THE MINE
Pennsylvania miners dig to place explosives under C.S.A. positions at Petersburg. The blast made a huge crater, but the defenders recovered and repelled the Union attack.

Losses	
Union:	(June 1864–May 1865) 42,000 casualties
C.S.A.:	(June 1864–May 1865) 28,000 casualties

SINKING A PRIVATEER

One by one, the U.S. Navy closed or blockaded Southern seaports. The C.S.A. had few fighting ships to challenge the Federal navy, which grew stronger thanks to Northern industrial might.

Foreign trade was essential to the South, but her commerce was strangled. Some fast Southern merchant ships became "blockade runners." They carried cotton to Europe, avoiding the blockading fleet. On their return trip they carried manufactured goods, munitions, cannon, and muskets. Other privately owned vessels were licensed as fighting ships by the C.S.A. Some won fame sinking Northern merchant vessels. The best "privateer"—also termed "commerce raider"—was the *Alabama*.

Built in Liverpool for the C.S.A. in 1862, she was considered the finest cruiser of her day. *Alabama* destroyed more than 60 merchant vessels and one Union warship. In June 1864, she and the sloop USS *Kearsarge* met in the French port of Cherbourg. The captains agreed to a duel at sea. Raphael Semmes captained the *Alabama*, and John A. Winslow the *Kearsarge*.

The ships were equal in size, with about the same number of guns. They were wooden-hulled, but the *Kearsarge* was protected by a layer of iron chains

A SAILOR'S CUTLASS

In the Civil War sailors still used cutlasses to fight off enemy boarders. This sword was the property of a Confederate navy lieutenant aboard the ironclad CSS *McRae*. Sailors also carried pistols and carbines.

UNION NAVY GUNNERS

Kearsarge gunners cheer as the stricken *Alabama* lowers her flag in defeat. Winslow praised his men for "coolness and fortitude" under fire. Only one Union sailor was killed.

Losses	
Union:	1 killed, 2 wounded
C.S.A.:	21 killed, 21 wounded

hung over her sides. They fought on June 19, with 15,000 French trying to see the fight from shore. The ships opened fire, and it soon became obvious the raider's crew lacked the skill of the navy gunners.

In less than two hours, Semmes had suffered many casualties, and his ship was sinking. He raised the white flag and leaped into the sea. Semmes and many survivors were rescued by a passing English steam yacht and brought to Britain.

DUEL IN FRENCH WATERS
Kearsarge came to Cherbourg to fight *Alabama*, which had put into the French harbor for repairs. Their battle was fought in the English Channel, within a few miles of the French coast. Spectators on shore and in nearby ships watched the battle.

THE LEADERSHIP

THE *ALABAMA*'S EXECUTIVE OFFICER was John M. Kell, who was rescued and brought to England. Kell later wrote about the raider. James S. Thornton was the *Kearsarge* executive officer. James R. Wheeler, acting master, ably commanded a Dahlgren gun.

RAPHAEL SEMMES (1809-1877)
Alabama's Raphael Semmes had Mexican War naval experience. Before the Civil War began, he went North and bought ammunition needed for the South. He rose to be a rear admiral and served until the end of the war.

"The flag that floats over you is that of a young republic! . . . Show the world that you know how to uphold it!"

—Semmes to his crew, going into action

Captain Winslow

JOHN A. WINSLOW (1811-1873)
Captain Winslow was a career naval officer, having enlisted in his teens. In his service as a gunboat commander with Farragut, he learned to use lengths of chain for armor. Winslow was promoted to commodore, and later to rear admiral.

"I saw now she was at our mercy, and a few more guns well-directed brought down her flag."

—Winslow, reporting on the engagement

A FIGHTING RETREAT

Grant went east to take charge of the Federal armies. Sherman replaced him as commander of operations in the western theater. Grant ordered Sherman to destroy the Confederate army and also methodically damage C.S.A. resources. In May 1864, Sherman set out to capture Atlanta, a major industrial center. Starting near Chattanooga, Sherman fought his way southward. His 100,000 men relentlessly pushed back Joseph Johnston. Johnston commanded 62,000 troops, a strong force, but Sherman kept making him withdraw to avoid being surrounded.

Johnston fought skillfully, but when he took up a strong position, Sherman usually moved around him instead of attacking. This forced Johnston to withdraw to block Sherman again farther south. There were several bloody engagements along the way, including at Resaca, New Hope Church, and Kennesaw Mountain. At this last position, Sherman attacked Johnston and was repulsed. Here, Johnston lost valuable corps commander Leonidas Polk, who was killed by an artillery salvo.

Johnston made another stand at the Chattahoochee River, but once again Sherman moved around him. In mid-July, Jefferson Davis interfered and replaced Johnston with John B. Hood. Attempting a counteroffensive, Hood was driven back into Atlanta. Several major actions occurred around the city as the two armies clashed. By late July, Sherman was laying siege to Atlanta. He had 85,000 men and Hood 42,000, including 5,000 local militia. For the next two months, ferocious struggles raged for possession of Atlanta.

THUNDER OF GUNS
An Alabama battery duels with Sherman's artillery in the Battle of Kennesaw Mountain, in June 1864. These artillerymen manhandled their guns up the steep mountainside to form a defense the Federals failed to storm.

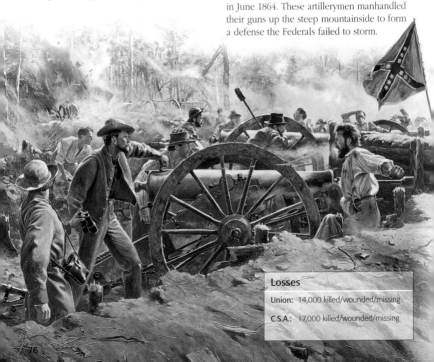

Losses	
Union:	14,000 killed/wounded/missing
C.S.A.:	17,000 killed/wounded/missing

Hole caused by wear, not bullets

SHERMAN'S CAMPAIGN HAT
Favorite hats of generals who went close to the front became battered and worn. Sherman's broad-brimmed hat served him until he reached Savannah. There a Union businessman gave him a new hat in exchange for this one.

THE ATLANTA CAMPAIGN
Sherman's army marched south from Chattanooga, Tennessee, into Georgia. Sherman moved around his opponents and forced them to withdraw. By late July, he had placed the Confederate army in Atlanta under siege.

███ SHERMAN
███ JOHNSTON

THE LEADERSHIP

SHERMAN HAD THREE COMMANDERS in George Thomas, James B. McPherson, and John M. Schofield. McPherson was killed in the Atlanta siege. Johnston's commanders were Leonidas Polk, William Hardee, and Benjamin F. Cheatham.

WILLIAM T. SHERMAN (1820–1910)
A West Pointer and Mexican War veteran, Sherman headed a Louisiana military school before the war. Many consider him the best Federal commander. In 1869, he succeeded Grant as commander-in-chief of the U.S. Army, a position he held until 1883.

"[W]ar, like the thunderbolt ... turns not aside even if the beautiful, the virtuous, and the charitable stand in its path."
—Sherman, on total war to destroy the Confederacy

LEONIDAS POLK (1806–1864)
A West Pointer and Episcopal bishop, General Polk fought in western theater actions that included Shiloh, Perryville, Stones River, and Chickamauga. The highly respected Polk was killed in the Atlanta campaign.

"[Jefferson] Davis condemns me for not fighting. General Sherman's testimony and that of the military cemetery at Marietta refute that charge."
—Johnston, after the war, about the Atlanta campaign

MARCHING THROUGH GEORGIA

On July 20, Hood counterattacked Sherman and was defeated at Peach Tree Creek, just outside Atlanta. General George Thomas's leadership was key to the Union victory. Two days later, Hood again attacked, in an engagement known as the Battle of Atlanta. The Confederates were repulsed, but Union general James McPherson was killed. Hood attacked again and again but was always driven back. Sherman's troops almost surrounded the city.

HENRY REPEATING RIFLE
This 16-shot repeating rifle belonged to an Illinois sharpshooter in the Atlanta campaign. Some Federal regiments were issued repeating rifles. This gave them devastating firepower compared to conventional one-shot army rifles.

To save his army, Hood evacuated Atlanta on September 1. He was determined to fight on. Sherman moved into Atlanta to rest and recuperate. Hood's Confederates invaded north toward Nashville. Sherman sent troops against him, but would not follow. He planned to march his main army to Savannah, then into South Carolina.

In mid-November, Sherman set out with more than 60,000 men in a march to the sea. First, he burned much of Atlanta, cutting off his army from communications and supplies. His men would live from the land, where food and forage were plentiful. Sherman thanked the South for its new policy of

FALL OF ATLANTA
General Sherman and an officer using field glasses consult the commander of an artillery battery during a bombardment of Atlanta in July 1864. General Hood's forces held out almost a month before evacuating the city.

Losses	
Union:	10,000 killed/wounded/missing
C.S.A.:	18,000 killed/wounded/missing

growing sweet potatoes and corn instead of only cotton. He destroyed what he did not take.

Sherman tore up railroads, burned plantations, and mercilessly stole and pillaged every step of the way. Fewer than 13,000 C.S.A. troops were left to stop him. Many thousands of liberated slaves followed Sherman in a column miles long. He took evacuated Savannah by mid-December and contacted the Union fleet there. The Carolinas campaign would follow. The region was defenseless, and even stubborn Charleston was abandoned.

▬▬▬ SHERMAN'S MARCH

MARCH TO THE SEA
Sherman's lean and tough army tore its way toward Savannah in late 1864 destroying everything in its path. Next, Sherman advanced into the Carolinas.

THE LEADERSHIP

WHEN HOOD'S MAIN ARMY WENT NORTH, William Hardee remained to oppose Sherman. Sherman's generals, Thomas and Schofield, went after Hood, and O.O. Howard took over McPherson's force. Beauregard later joined Hardee in the Carolinas.

JOHN B. HOOD (1831-1879)
A professional soldier, Hood was a West Pointer. He was brilliant and aggressive leading brigades or divisions. Commanding a full army was beyond his ability, however. His battle wounds left him with one crippled arm and an amputated leg.

"I was not so much pained by the fall of Atlanta as by the . . . retreat, which . . . would further demoralize the army and renew desertions."

—from Hood's memoirs after the war

JAMES B. MCPHERSON (1828-1864)
General McPherson was a West Point graduate and instructor. He was Grant's chief engineer in the western theater. He became a division commander then took over the Army of the Tennessee. McPherson was killed during the Battle of Atlanta when he rode into enemy skirmishers on a forest road.

"[H]ow precious the country to us all, who have paid for its preservation with such a price."

—General O.O. Howard, lamenting the death of McPherson

DAMN THE TORPEDOES!

The Confederacy had few large seaports left by the summer of 1864 because the Union had captured most of them. The C.S.A. desperately needed overseas trade, especially to buy armaments. One of the most important remaining seaports was Mobile, Alabama, home port for blockade runners. Union troops were not near enough to strike Mobile from land. The crucial attack came, instead, by sea.

In August, Union admiral David Farragut attacked Mobile's outer harbor forts. He sent his 14 warships and four gunboats steaming in two lines past the forts. Farragut had successfully run past enemy batteries at New Orleans, Port Hudson, and Vicksburg. A layer of chain cables protected the sides of his wooden ships. At the opening of the battle on August 5, his lead ironclad, the *Tecumseh*, was sunk by an underwater mine, also called a

THE LEADERSHIP

CAPTAIN TUNIS A. CRAVEN OF THE *Tecumseh* was so eager to attack the *Tennessee* that he went off his intended course and into the mines. C.S.A. general Richard L. Page did not surrender Fort Morgan until its walls had been blown apart.

FRANKLIN BUCHANAN (1800-1874)
Admiral Buchanan had been the first superintendent of the U.S. Naval Academy. He was a career officer before joining the C.S.A. He captained the ironclad *Virginia*, sinking the *Congress* at Hampton Roads. Fighting against him on the *Congress* was his own brother.

"Well, Johnston, they've got me. You'll have to look after her now."

—Buchanan, wounded, telling an officer to take command of the *Tennessee*

DAVID G. FARRAGUT (1801-1870)
After successes on the Mississippi, Admiral Farragut had a hero's welcome in New York City. After the Battle of Mobile Bay, Farragut was awarded $50,000 by the citizens of New York to buy a home there. In 1865, he was among the first Northerners to enter Richmond.

"When I reached the upmost round of the ladder, the vessel seemed to drop from under me."

—The last officer, on escaping the sinking *Tecumseh*

torpedo. Farragut commanded his fleet to push right through the mines.

"Damn the torpedoes!" he ordered. "Go ahead! Full speed!"

Only 21 of the *Tecumseh*'s crew of 114 were saved. Farragut took on the small enemy fleet and the ironclad ram, *Tennessee*. She was the most powerful enemy vessel. Surrounded by Union ships and gunboats, she was bombarded and rammed again and again. The *Tennessee* was commanded by Franklin Buchanan, a pre-war friend of Farragut's. Soon, she was badly damaged, unable to steer or to fire her guns, and Buchanan was wounded. The *Tennessee* surrendered, and in a few weeks Farragut took the harbor forts.

The city of Mobile did not fall until April 1865, but she was no longer a home port for blockade runners. Only Wilmington, North Carolina, remained as a major C.S.A. seaport. In losing her ports, the South lost vital communication and trade with other countries.

ALABAMA
FLORIDA
MOBILE
FT. POWELL
Mobile Bay
FT. GAINES
FT. MORGAN
GULF OF MEXICO

▬▬ FARRAGUT

PASSING THE FORTS
David Farragut did not hesitate to run his ships past Mobile Bay's outer forts. He blasted his way into the bay and defeated the small C.S.A. fleet there.

AN IRONCLAD SHIELD
Farragut used his ironclad gunboats to protect his wooden-hulled warships. The ironclads steamed in a line between the wooden ships and Fort Morgan's guns. The C.S.A. ram *Tennessee,* counterattacking at bottom center, is soon to be captured.

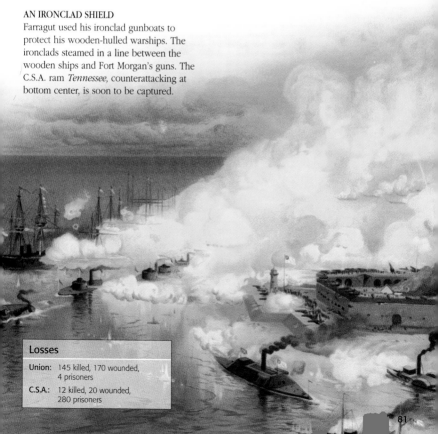

Losses
Union: 145 killed, 170 wounded, 4 prisoners

C.S.A.: 12 killed, 20 wounded, 280 prisoners

BURNING THE SHENANDOAH

The Shenandoah Valley meant much to the Southern war effort. It was a source of food and also was an invasion route aimed at Washington. In mid-1864, Lee sent Jubal Early to drive out Union troops in the northern part of the valley. Early did so and then advanced his 8,000 men on Washington itself.

Grant's main army was massed near Richmond, so mainly invalids and supply clerks were left to face Early. What saved Washington were its strong fortifications. Though weakly manned, the works were so formidable that Early turned away from them.

The U.S. government was shocked by the danger. Grant now had to drive Early out of the Shenandoah. He sent his tough cavalry commander, Philip H. Sheridan, to defeat Early. Grant instructed Sheridan to destroy all crops and supplies so the C.S.A. would never get them.

Sheridan and his 30,000 men efficiently carried out their orders.

THE LEADERSHIP

GENERAL JOHN G. BARNARD IS A LITTLE-KNOWN hero of the Civil War. The Union's chief military engineer, Barnard designed Washington's defenses so well that Early dared not attack them.

"[The fortifications were] exceedingly strong [and] as far as the eye could reach, the works seemed to be...impregnable."

—Early, on his reconnaissance of Washington's defenses

JUBAL A. EARLY (1816–1894)

A West Pointer and Mexican War veteran, Early was a top leader in the Confederate army. Yet he was outmaneuvered by the hard-hitting Sheridan in the Shenandoah. Rather than surrender in 1865, Early went to Mexico, then Canada. He later returned to practice law in his native Virginia.

"Take all provisions, forage, and stock [and whatever] cannot be consumed, destroy."

—Grant's orders to Sheridan

GEORGE A. CUSTER (1839–1876)

Though last in his West Point class, Custer was a gallant cavalry leader. A general at 23, he was in almost every battle of the Army of the Potomac. Wounded only once, he had 11 horses killed under him. Custer led a cavalry division in the Shenandoah campaign.

They defeated Early's enlarged force of 14,000 troops at Winchester in September. Then Sheridan burned farms and fields and slaughtered livestock. His ruthless destruction of the Shenandoah compared with Sherman's devastating march through Georgia.

In October, Early surprised Sheridan's army, camped at Cedar Creek. The battle went against the Federals until Sheridan rode in and rallied his men. He had galloped 20 miles to reach the action—a feat known as "Sheridan's Ride." Early was forced to retreat from the Shenandoah, which remained in Union hands for the rest of the war. Sheridan continued his destruction. He said a crow flying over the valley that winter would have to carry its own supplies on its back.

EARLY'S RAID ON WASHINGTON

Not only did Early drive Union forces out of the Shenandoah Valley, but he advanced on Washington. Early reached Fort Stevens, just four miles from the White House. Finding the defensive works around the capital too strong to attack, he withdrew.

EARLY'S RAID

SHERIDAN'S RIDE

General Philip Sheridan gallops past cheering Union soldiers after riding 20 miles nonstop to reach the battlefield of Cedar Creek on October 19. Sheridan turned retreat into a victory that ended C.S.A. control of the Shenandoah Valley.

Losses

Union: approximately 11,300 killed/wounded/missing

C.S.A.: approximately 8,500 killed/wounded/missing

HOOD'S ARMY IS BROKEN

With Atlanta in Sherman's hands, Hood saw only one choice—keep on the offensive. In September, he took the 39,000 men left in his Army of the Tennessee and struck northward. He planned to cut Sherman's communications and invade Tennessee. As a border state, Tennessee had many Confederate sympathizers. Hood hoped thousands would rise to join him. If so, then Sherman would have to abandon Georgia and return north.

Sherman sent George Thomas up to Nashville to prepare for Hood. Schofield also went northward, trying to outrun Hood to key crossroads and railroad junctions. These two armies clashed at Columbia and Spring Hill with a few hundred casualties on each side. A full-scale battle erupted on November 30 at Franklin, 18 miles from Nashville.

Hood sent 25,000 massed troops charging across the open fields, their tattered red battle flags flying. They met murderous fire, but troops under General Patrick Cleburne broke through the Union line. A counterattack by Union reserves hurled them back, killing Cleburne. The surviving Confederates withdrew after darkness fell.

Hood had lost 7,000 men, but he pressed on desperately toward Nashville. He reached the edge of the city on December 1 with 25,000 weary, hungry men. Thomas and Schofield

JUST BEFORE DEATH
General Cleburne gallops forward in an ill-fated assault at Franklin, Tennessee. Cleburne's men broke into the Union defenses by charging close behind hundreds of enemy soldiers fleeing into their own lines. An enemy counterattack killed him.

Losses

Union: 5,300 killed/wounded/missin

C.S.A. 11,000 killed/wounded/miss

had 50,000 well-supplied and rested troops to face him. Thomas was in command of the Union forces. On December 15, he attacked Hood's thinly spread units and drove them back. Hood made another stand the next day, but the next Union assault routed him completely.

The proud Confederate Army of the Tennessee was destroyed. Those who could, fled south. Hood had suffered another 6,700 casualties. The Union's total campaign loss was 5,300.

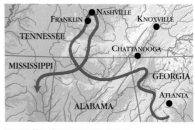

▬▬▬ HOOD'S INVASION AND RETREAT

A DESPERATE RUSH NORTH
John Hood's C.S.A. Army of the Tennessee brought war back to Nashville. Hood fought his way to the city's gates, then was defeated and driven back.

THE LEADERSHIP

THE FAMOUS C.S.A. CAVALRY GENERAL Nathan B. Forrest was with Hood. Forrest was considered one of the South's finest soldiers. Yet he could not prevent Union cavalry under General James H. Wilson from harassing Hood's beaten retreating army.

PATRICK R. CLEBURNE (1828-1864)
Born in Ireland, General Cleburne was one of the finest and most courageous generals of the Confederacy. He had been an officer in the British Army before emigrating to Arkansas. Cleburne fought at Shiloh, Perryville, Stones River, Chickamauga, Chattanooga, and the Atlanta campaign. He was called "Stonewall of the West."

"I never saw men put in such a terrible position as Cleburne's division was in...."

—Union soldier describing Franklin, with Cleburne under fire

JOHN M. SCHOFIELD (1831-1906)
Schofield graduated from West Point, and later taught there. He rose from artillery captain to be major general commanding the Army of the Ohio. Schofield fought throughout the western theater. After the war, he became West Point's superintendent and then the general-in-chief of the army.

"The whole Northwest was saved from an invasion that... would have more than neutralized all Sherman's successes in Georgia."

—General Henry Stone, Thomas's staff officer

Grant Traps Lee, Pursuit to Appomattox

The year opened with C.S.A. arms on the defensive. Yet the South would not give up. The Confederacy hoped to inflict so many casualties that a peace treaty, not surrender, would end the war.

Many veterans of both armies were willing to fight to the death, with or without supplies. The North's industrial might provided its troops with uniforms, weapons, and food. The embattled South could hardly find the barest supplies for its men.

Sherman was advancing into the Carolinas against Johnston, and Grant besieged Lee at Petersburg—key to defending Richmond. Lee fought hard, but did not have enough

CHARGING CAVALRY
Sheridan's cavalry attacks war-weary Virginia infantry at the Battle of Five Forks on April 1. The Southern troops were part of Lee's army, retreating from Richmond, which finally fell to Grant on April 3.

January	February	March	April
Fort Fisher, North Carolina, falls to Union forces	Failure of peace conference between Lincoln and C.S.A. Vice President Alexander Stephens	Lincoln inaugurated for a second term	Grant breaks Lee's lines at Petersburg
Sherman begins campaign into Carolinas		A last C.S.A. offensive at Petersburg fails	Fall of Richmond
			Lincoln enters Richmond

men or supplies. Grant seemed to have an endless source of reinforcements. By April, he drove Lee from Petersburg and captured Richmond. Sherman also had defeated Johnston at Bentonville, North Carolina.

Lee tried to escape to fight again, but Grant did not let him. The Federals pressed Lee's Army of Northern Virginia on all sides until it had no choice but to surrender at Appomattox on April 9. Johnston gave up a few weeks later. The C.S.A. soldiers were paroled and allowed to go home, and victory bells rang out across the North.

Then President Lincoln was assassinated on April 14, and the Union went into deep mourning.

The remaining Confederate forces gave up, one by one, and C.S.A. President Jefferson Davis was taken into Federal custody. The last Confederate fighting force surrendered to General Edward R. Canby at Mobile on May 26. The war was over.

AFTER DEFEAT
Northern photographer Mathew B. Brady visited desolate Richmond soon after her fall in April 1865. He photographed these ruins of a factory complex. This area would soon be rebuilt after the war.

THE DEATH OF LINCOLN

In April 1865, the North was overjoyed by Lee's surrender. Yet bitter Southern sympathizers wanted revenge. One was John Wilkes Booth, an actor in his mid-twenties. On April 14, Lincoln attended a play at Ford's Theater, and Booth entered the president's private box and shot him in the head. Booth leaped down to the stage, shouting, "The South is avenged!" Lincoln died the next morning. Booth escaped the theater, but was pursued into Virginia and shot down a few days later.

A FATAL SHOT
John Wilkes Booth assassinates President Lincoln, who is seated next to his wife. Booth was part of a conspiracy ring.

April (continued)	May	November	December
Lee surrenders to Grant at Appomattox Court House	Last C.S.A. forces under Richard Taylor and Kirby Smith surrender	Last Confederate ocean raider, CSS *Shenandoah*, turns herself over to British at Liverpool, England	13th Amendment to the Constitution is passed, abolishing slavery.
Lincoln is assassinated			
Johnston surrenders	Jefferson Davis captured by Union troops		

RICHMOND BURNS

The nine-month siege of Petersburg wore down the outnumbered Confederate defenders. They were hungry and poorly supplied and equipped. The Federals, on the other hand, were growing stronger as the siege continued. They were supplied through a massive base at City Point, Virginia on the James River.

In late March, Lee attempted an offensive by attacking Fort Stedman, a Union strongpoint. He took the fort, but an enemy counterattack recaptured it. Lee lost almost 5,000 men, and the Union lost 2,000. On March 30, Grant launched an assault on Lee's right wing near the crossroads called Five Forks.

Sheridan's cavalry led the operation, joining General Gouverneur Warren's corps. Lee sent George Pickett to stop the relentless Federal advance, but the C.S.A. troops were steadily driven back. Pickett's counterattacks failed, and by the time he withdrew, he had lost more than 8,000 men. The Union lost fewer than 1,000.

On April 2, Grant attacked and broke through the enemy defenses at Petersburg. Veteran C.S.A. general A.P. Hill was killed in this engagement. Lee had to withdraw from Petersburg and could no longer defend Richmond. His army marched westward, planning to join with Joseph Johnston's remaining force. The Confederate government evacuated the capital, and President

RICHMOND BURNING
Cavalry and carriages of Confederate officials flee Richmond, in flames across the James River, on April 2. The column is heading westward to avoid capture by the closing pincers of Grant's army.

Losses	
Union:	830 killed/wounded/missing
C.S.A.:	2950 killed/wounded
	5,200 prisoners

Davis ordered military equipment, government arsenals, mills, and factories destroyed. These were set on fire. Soon Richmond was ablaze, rocked by explosions as munitions went up. Fires raced out of control, and thousands of citizens became homeless. There was mob violence, drunkenness, and looting that night. The next morning, April 3, Federal troops marched in and pulled down the Confederate flag from the capitol building.

Lincoln came to Richmond the next day. He rode through the still-smoking city in an open coach and visited Davis's home. For a moment, Lincoln sat quietly at the desk of the defeated Confederate president.

VIRGINIA
RICHMOND
James River
CITY POINT
PETERSBURG
FIVE FORKS

◼◼◼◼ PICKETT   ◼◼◼◼ SHERIDAN

PRELUDE TO DEFEAT
Lee's army held on at Petersburg, but Philip Sheridan's cavalry and Union infantry destroyed their right wing at Five Forks. This was the last major battle of the campaign.

THE LEADERSHIP

GENERALS GEORGE CUSTER AND RANALD MACKENZIE led Union cavalry at Five Forks against cavalry general Fitzhugh Lee, nephew of Robert E. Lee. Union general Horatio G. Wright's corps broke the Petersburg defenses.

GOUVERNEUR WARREN (1830–1882)
A mapmaker and engineer, Warren was a West Pointer. He served in the eastern campaigns with distinction. Sheridan accused him of not being aggressive at Five Forks. Warren demanded an inquiry, and Sheridan was proven wrong. Warren earned many battlefield honors, including a statue at Gettysburg.

"Then we saw a dense column of infantry march by, seemingly without end; we heard the[ir] cheers…and then we turned and slowly rode on our way."
—A Southern captain observes Richmond's occupation

WILLIAM J. PEGRAM (1841–1865)
Law student William Pegram enlisted in the C.S.A. Army as a private. He soon became an artillery captain, his gallantry and skill bringing him to Lee's attention. Pegram commanded artillery in almost every battle Lee fought, from Seven Days' through Petersburg. Pegram was killed at Five Forks, a few days after the death of his famous brother, General John Pegram.

"He is at rest now, and we who are left are the ones to suffer."
—Lee, upon hearing of A.P. Hill's death

LEE SURRENDERS TO GRANT

If Lee and his 50,000 troops joined Joseph Johnston, they could number more than 65,000 men. Of course, they would also have to face Sherman, who was chasing Johnston.

Grant, with 112,000 troops, gave Lee no rest. Union cavalry under Sheridan and Custer dashed around, blocking roads and attacking supply wagons and trains. The exhausted, starving Southern troops were hit at several places. The hardest was at Sayler's Creek on April 6, where 8,000 Confederates fought back savagely, hand-to-hand. They were all captured, and with them six generals, including the formidable Richard Ewell.

On April 7, Sheridan's cavalry placed itself across Lee's line of retreat. Lee had no food, his men were too exhausted to fight their way out, and many were deserting. Grant sent Lee a letter calling for surrender.

Awaiting Lee's reply, Grant stayed at a hotel in Farmville. At nightfall, Horatio Wright's weary corps came slogging through after a long day's march. When they noticed Grant watching them from the hotel porch,

MEMENTOS OF A HERO
Gauntlets and shoulder straps worn by General Joshua L. Chamberlain, awarded the Medal of Honor for bravery at Gettysburg. Chamberlain was an example of the best in the American citizen soldier.

THE LAST SALUTE
Lee's army marches out to lay down arms at Appomattox Court House on April 12, 1865. General Joshua Chamberlain and his troops salute them, and C.S.A. general John Gordon returns the salute.

Losses

Union:	1,316 killed, 7,750 wounded, 1,714 missing
C.S.A.:	6,266 killed/wounded, 45,000 captured/missing

they straightened up and cheered. A spring came into their step, many lit torches, their bands played, and flags fluttered. Bonfires flared up along the street as thousands of soldiers passed in a spontaneous grand review.

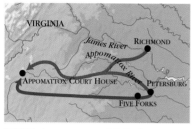

Lee's retreat   Grant

A veteran general considered it one of the most inspiring moments of the war.

Lee soon replied to Grant, asking for surrender terms.

Grant and Lee met in the hamlet of Appomattox Court House on April 9. Lee surrendered 27,000 men, who were paroled to go home. Johnston surrendered to Sherman on April 26.

RETREAT AND PURSUIT
Grant's cavalry blocked Lee's escape route. On April 9, 1865, Lee surrendered at Appomattox Court House.

THE LEADERSHIP

AMONG THOSE AT THE CEREMONY, held in the Wilmer McLean house, was Grant's staff, cavalry generals Sheridan, Custer, and Wesley Merritt, and corps commander Edward O. Ord. Lee had only his military secretary, Colonel Charles Marshall.

"The results of the last week must convince you of the hopelessness of further resistance . . . in this struggle."

—Grant to Lee, proposing surrender

"There is nothing left . . . but to go and see General Grant, and I had rather die a thousand deaths."

—Lee, before his surrender

THE BLUE AND THE GRAY

UNION LEADERS

JOHN G. BARNARD
Chief Engineer in charge
of Washington defenses,
superintendent of West
Point before the war.

WILLIAM F. BARTLETT
Massachusetts general; lost a
leg, but led 49th Massachusetts
and raised the 57th; wounded
three more times.

DAVID B. BIRNEY
Southern-born lawyer
and son of an abolitionist;
raised 23rd Pennsylvania
regiment at his own expense.

DON CARLOS BUELL
West Pointer; won honors for
bravery in Mexican war;
replaced for being too cautious;
Grant respected his ability.

BENJAMIN F. BUTLER
Massachusetts politician;
incompetent field commander,
and unpopular military
governor of New Orleans.

JOHN GIBBON
West Point artillery instructor;
wounded leading troops at
Fredericksburg and Gettysburg;
three brothers fought for C.S.A.

HENRY W. HALLECK
West Pointer and Napoleonic
wars scholar; Lincoln's
military advisor and, later,
chief of staff.

HERMAN HAUPT
West Pointer and railroad
engineer, in charge of
transportation and construction
of military railroads.

PHILIP KEARNY
Lost arm in Mexican War; a
distinguished general in
Peninsular Campaign; killed
at Chantilly in 1862.

"I believe it to be the duty of every one to unite in the restoration of the country. . . ."

—Robert E. Lee, September 1865

CONFEDERATE LEADERS

JOSEPH R. ANDERSON
West Pointer and artillery officer; commanded brigade on Peninsula, wounded at Frayser's Farm.

JUDAH P. BENJAMIN
Former U.S. senator; was C.S.A. attorney general, then secretary of war and secretary of state.

JOHN C. BRECKINRIDGE
Former congressman and U.S. vice president; C.S.A. general until 1865, then secretary of war.

BENJAMIN F. CHEATHAM
General in western theater, became corps commander; surrendered with Joseph Johnston in 1865.

NATHAN B. FORREST
General and leader of famed mounted raids in western theater; fought until the end of the war.

WADE HAMPTON
Raised Hampton Legion in 1861; a general in Lee's campaigns; went home rather than surrender.

FITZHUGH LEE
West Pointer, C.S.A. cavalry general under Lee; seriously wounded in 1864; returned to action.

STEPHEN D. LEE
West Point artillerist, bombarded Fort Sumter in 1861; led troops in eastern and western theaters.

LAFAYETTE MCLAWS
Attended University of Virginia and West Point; fought in East and West; in Johnston's last campaign.

UNION LEADERS

MONTGOMERY C. MEIGS
West Point engineer and artillerist; U.S. quartermaster general in charge of supplying the armies.

WINFIELD SCOTT
Elderly general-in-chief of the army in 1861, conceived plan to crush South by occupying the Mississippi.

WILLIAM HENRY SEWARD
Former N.Y. governor and senator; Lincoln's secretary of state; wounded in 1865 assassination plot.

EDWIN M. STANTON
Union secretary of war; a Kentuckian, he opposed slavery but defended rights of slave holders.

GIDEON WELLES
Lincoln's secretary of the navy; effective administrator despite having no naval experience.

CONFEDERATE LEADERS

STEPHEN R. MALLORY
C.S.A. secretary of the navy; a U.S. senator from Florida, he resigned to join Jefferson Davis's cabinet.

JOHN S. MOSBY
Led Partisan Rangers; western Virginia was called "Mosby's Confederacy"; disbanded his men rather than surrender.

ALEXANDER H. STEPHENS
Former U.S. congressman; key figure in secession movement, became C.S.A. vice president.

RICHARD TAYLOR
Son of President Zachary Taylor; general in East and West; one of last commanders to surrender.

ROBERT A. TOOMBS
Former U.S. congressman and senator; C.S.A. general and secretary of state; wounded at Antietam.

INDEX

ACKNOWLEDGMENTS

Media Projects, Inc., and DK Publishing, Inc., offer their grateful thanks to: artist and collector Don Troiani, Historical Art Prints, www.historicalartprints.com; historical consultant Brian Pohanka; Anne Richtarik of the Mercer Museum; and Rob Stokes and James Burmester for relief mapping and cartography.

Photography and Art Credits
(t=top; b=bottom; l=left; r=right; c=center; a=above)
Courtesy of Appomattox Court House National Historic Park: 11cr, 91b. **Battles and Leaders of the Civil War**: 20cl, 21cl, 24cl, 26cl, 26br, 48cl, 93tr, 93cl, 93cr, 93bl, 93bc, 93br, 94bl, 94br. **Confederate Memorial Hall**: 4t, 5cl, 18cr, 25cl, 30c, 47tr. **The Museum of the Confederacy, Richmond, Virginia**: 89br. **Gettysburg National Military Park**: 49cr, 74c. **Photographer Dave King**: 17r. **Library of Congress**: 6–7b, 7cr, 8t, 9b, 10bl, 10cr, 11tl, 11bl, 14c, 16b, 19bl, 20b, 21b, 22–23b, 22cr, 23cr, 24b, 25b, 27b, 29cl, 30b, 31br, 34cr, 35cl, 36br, 36cl, 39br, 44–45b, 44tr, 45cr, 46b, 47cl, 47br, 48br, 49b, 51cl, 51br, 52br, 57cl, 57br, 58bl, 59cl, 59br, 60b, 61cl, 62b, 63cl, 63br, 64c, 65cr, 66cl, 66br, 67b, 68br, 70b, 71cl, 71br, 73br, 74b, 75cl, 75br, 77cl, 77br, 78b, 79br, 80cl, 80br, 81b, 82br, 83b, 85br, 86tr, 87cr, 88b, 89cl, 92tl, 92tr, 92cr, 92bl, 92bc, 92br,

93tl, 93c, 94tl, 94tc, 94tr, 94acl, 94acr, 94cl, 94c, 94cr. **Courtesy Commonwealth of Massachusetts**: 8c (photo by Douglas Christian), 43c. **Collection of the Mercer Museum of the Bucks County Historical Society**: 34b. **National Archives**: 14–15b, 17cl, 17br, 19cr, 23cl, 31cl, 33br, 41br, 42br, 55br, 64–65b, 72cl, 73cl, 86–87b, 92tc, 92cl, 92c, 93tc. **Collection of Lloyd Ostendorf courtesy of Mrs. Rita Ostendorf**: 33cl. **The State Museum of Pennsylvania, Pennsylvania Historical and Museum Commission**: 56c. **Paintings by Don Troiani, www.historicalartprints.com**: 1c, 2–3c, 13br, 18b, 28b, 32b, 37b, 38b, 40b, 43b, 50b, 53b, 54b, 56b, 69b, 72b, 76b, 84b, 90b. **Courtesy of Don Troiani, www.historicalartprints.com**: 4b, 5t, 5cr, 5bl, 9t, 15t, 33tr, 38t, 41tr, 50c, 53c, 54cl, 58br, 59cr, 60c, 62t, 67c, 69cr, 78c, 90c. **U.S. Army Military History Institute**: 27c, 77tl. **Cook Collection, Valentine Museum**: 29br, 35br, 39cl, 41cl, 42cl, 52cl, 55cl, 58cl, 61br, 68cl, 79cl, 82cl, 85cl. **U.S. Military Academy at West Point**: 15cr.

Cover Credits: **Civil War Times Illustrated :** front tla. **Confederate Memorial Hall, New Orleans, LA**: front br, front cr. **Gettysburg National Military Park**: back. **Library of Congress**: front cl. **Slimfilms, New York, NY**: map, front c. **Courtesy of Don Troiani, www.historicalartprints.com**: front flap, back flap.